ACROSS THE UNIVERSE

By JOHN LENNON and PAUL McCARTNEY

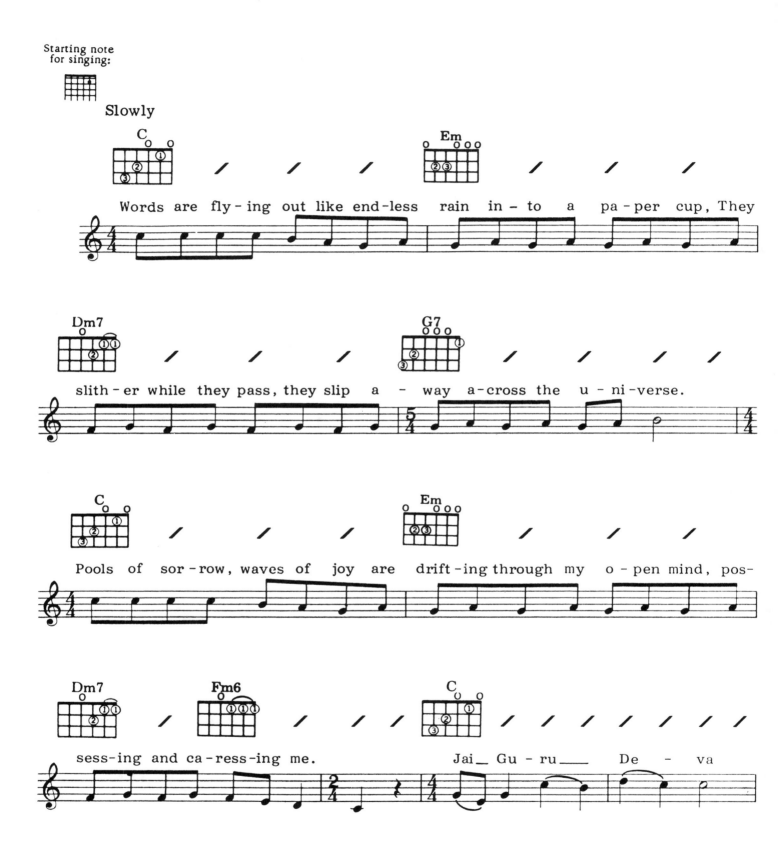

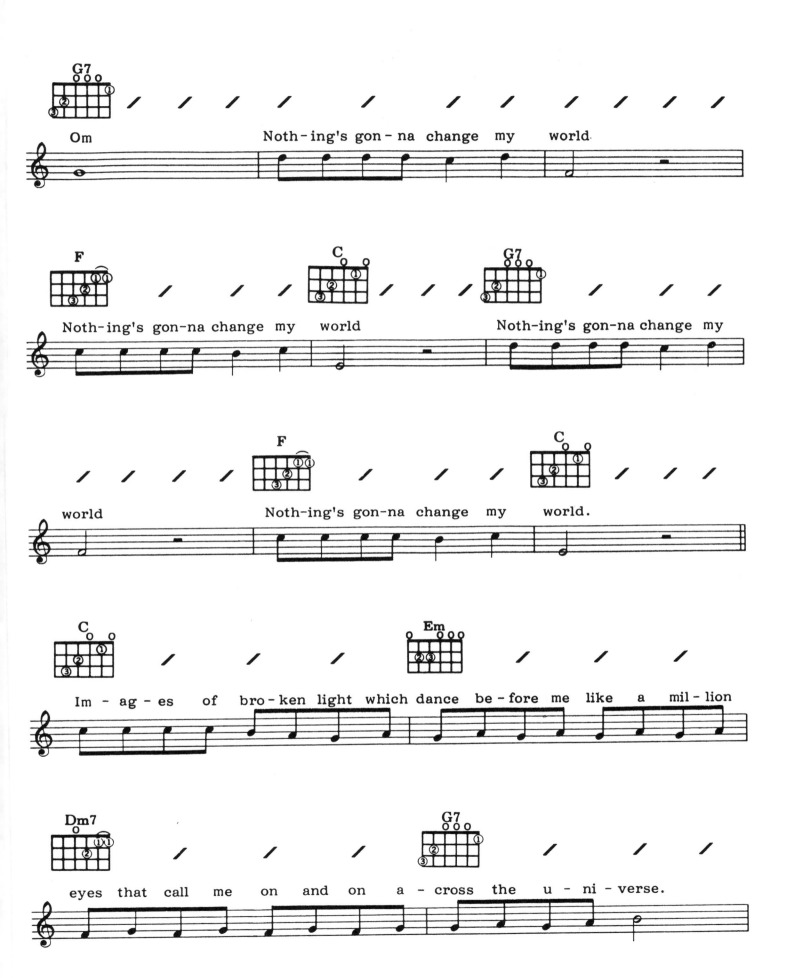

6

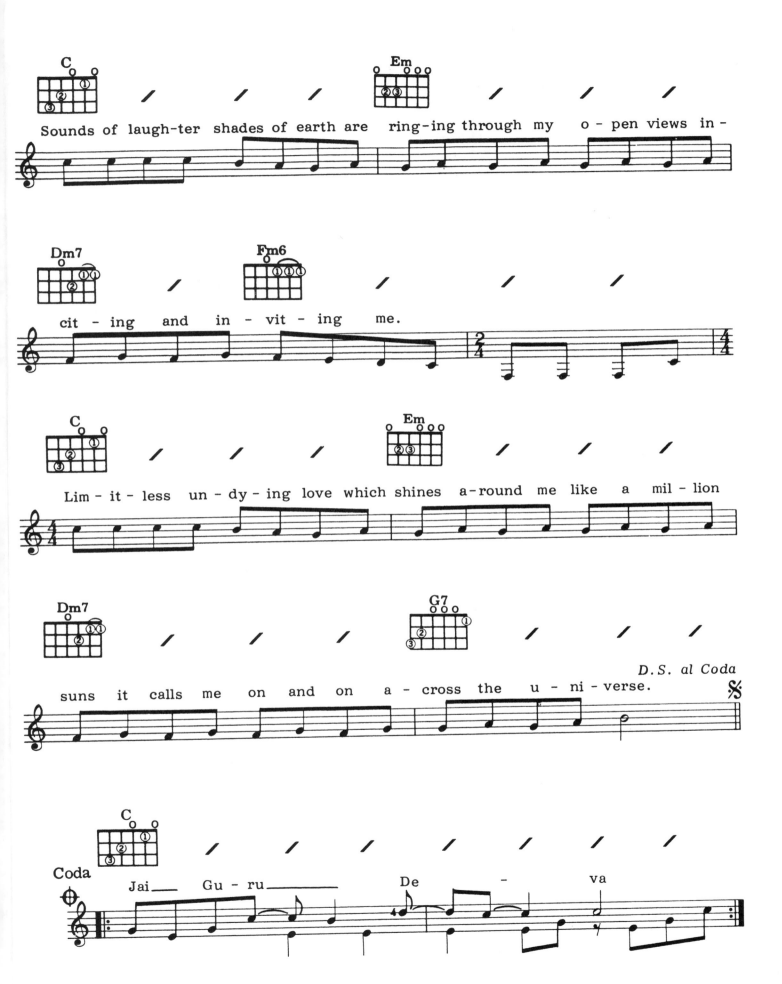

ALL I'VE GOT TO DO

By JOHN LENNON and PAUL McCARTNEY

ALL MY LOVING

By JOHN LENNON and PAUL McCARTNEY

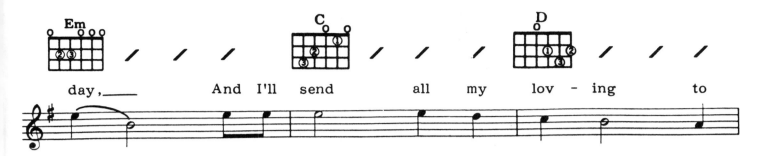

day,_____ And I'll send all my lov - ing to

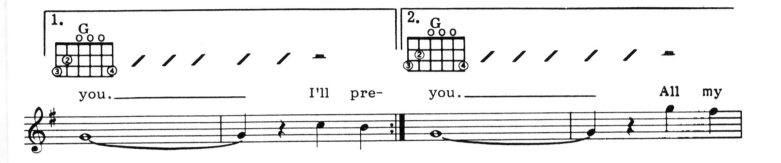

1. you._____ I'll pre-   **2.** you._____ All my

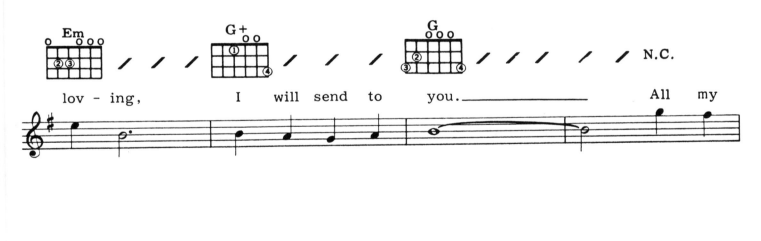

lov - ing,   I will send to   you._____   N.C.   All my

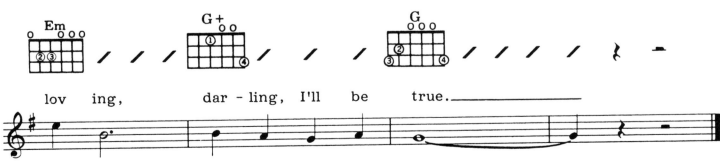

lov ing,   dar - ling, I'll be   true._____

ALL TOGETHER NOW

By JOHN LENNON and PAUL McCARTNEY

All to-geth - er now, All to-geth - er

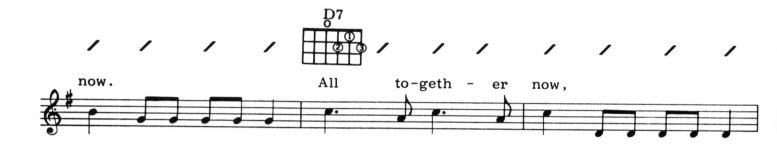

now. All to-geth - er now,

All to-geth - er now. All to -

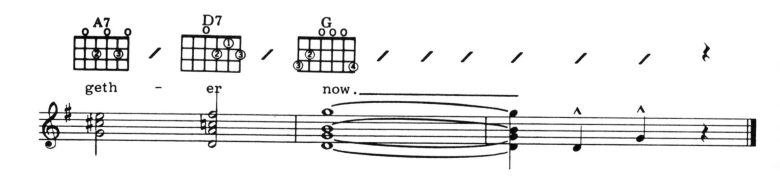

geth - er now.

BEING FOR THE BENEFIT OF MR. KITE

By JOHN LENNON and PAUL McCARTNEY

2. The celebrated Mr. K. performs his feat on Saturday at Bishopsgate.
   The Hendersons will dance and sing as Mr. Kite flies through the ring; don't be late.
   Messrs. K. and H. assure the public their production will be second to none.
   And, of course, Henry the Horse dances the waltz.

3. The band begins at ten to six when Mr. K. performs his tricks without a sound.
   And Mr. H. will demonstrate ten somersets he'll undertake on solid ground.
   Having been some days in preparation, a splendid time is guaranteed for all.
   And tonight Mr. Kite is topping the bill.

ALL YOU NEED IS LOVE

By JOHN LENNON and PAUL McCARTNEY

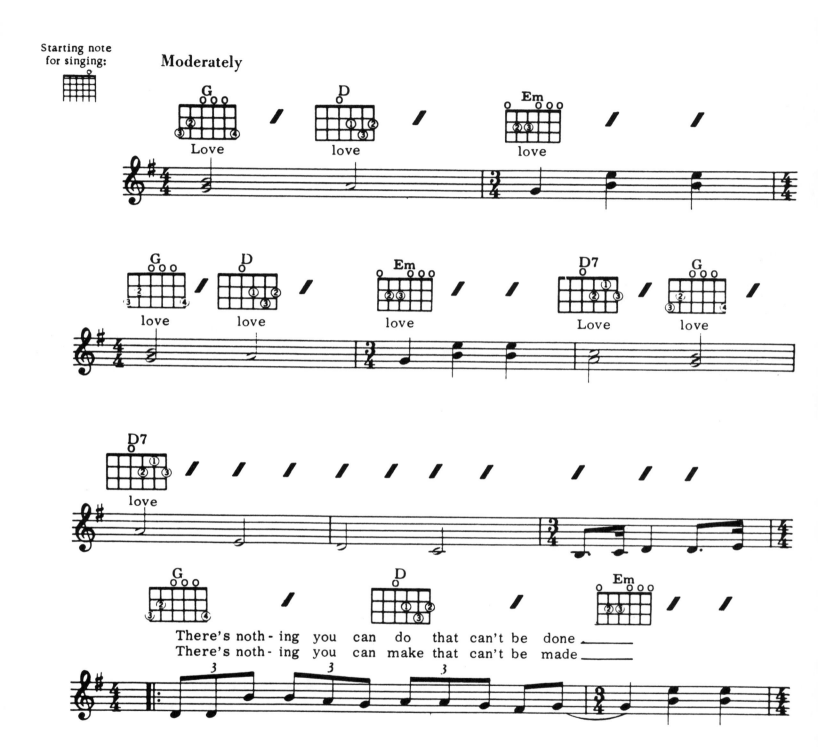

Starting note for singing:

Moderately

Love love love

love love love Love love

love

There's noth-ing you can do that can't be done ____
There's noth-ing you can make that can't be made ____

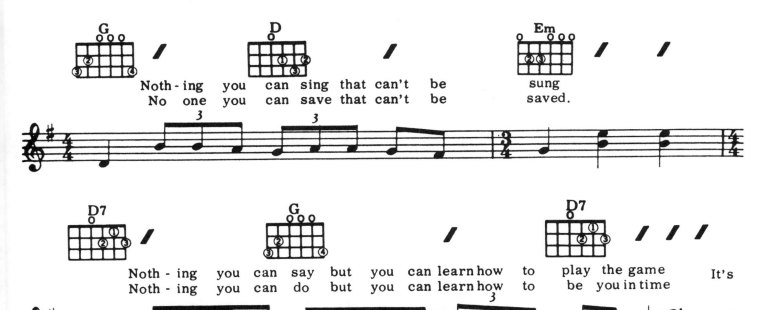

Noth - ing you can sing that can't be sung
No one you can save that can't be saved.

Noth - ing you can say but you can learn how to play the game It's
Noth - ing you can do but you can learn how to be you in time

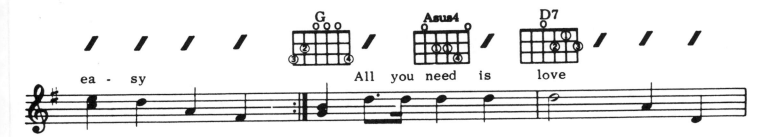

ea - sy   All you need is love

All you need is love.   All you need is

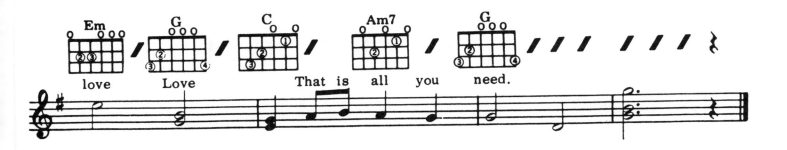

love   Love   That is all you   need.

AND I LOVE HER

By JOHN LENNON and PAUL McCARTNEY

Starting note
for singing:

I give her all my love, That's all I
She gives me ev-'ry-thing, And ten-der

do; ___ And if you saw my love
ly; ___ The kiss my lov-er brings

1.
You'd love her too, ___ I ___ love her. ___
She brings to me, ___ And I

2.
love her. ___

A love like

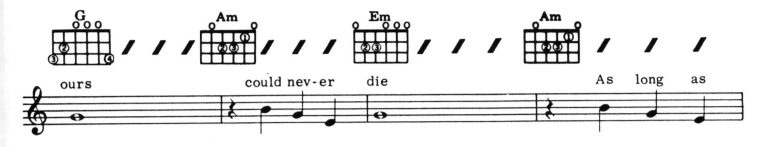

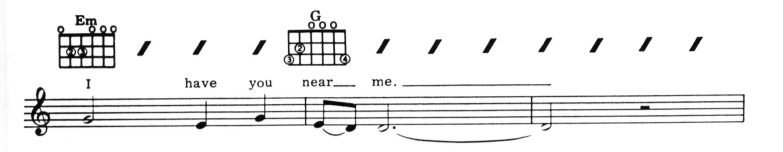

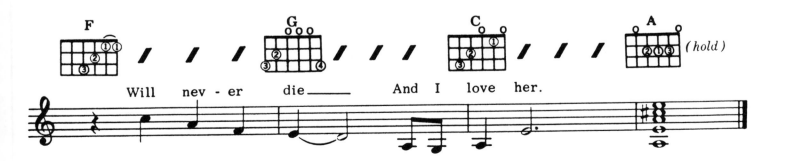

AND YOUR BIRD CAN SING

By JOHN LENNON and PAUL McCARTNEY

D. S. 𝄉 al Coda ⊕

'round.

You tell me that you've heard ev - 'ry sound there is and your bird can sing but you can't hear me, you can't hear me!

Coda ⊕

ANOTHER GIRL

By JOHN LENNON and PAUL McCARTNEY

2. She's sweeter than all the girls, and I've met quite a few.
   Nobody in all the world can do what she can do.
   And so I'm tellin' you, this time you'd better stop.
   For I have got *(etc.)*

3. I don't wanna say that I've been unhappy with you,
   But as from today, well, I've seen somebody that's new.
   I ain't no fool and I don't take what I don't want.
   For I have got *(etc.)*

Starting note for singing:

ANYTIME AT ALL

By JOHN LENNON and PAUL McCARTNEY

Rather fast

An-y time at all, _____ An-y time at all, _____ An-y time at all, _____ All you got-ta do is call _____ and I'll _____ be there.

If you need some-bod-y to love, _____ Just look in-to my eyes,
If the sun has fad-ed a-way _____ I'll try to make it shine;

I'll _____ be there _____ to make you feel _____
There is noth-in' _____ I _____ won't _____

BABY, YOU'RE A RICH MAN

By JOHN LENNON and PAUL McCARTNEY

BABY'S IN BLACK

By JOHN LENNON and PAUL McCARTNEY

Starting note
for singing:

Rather fast

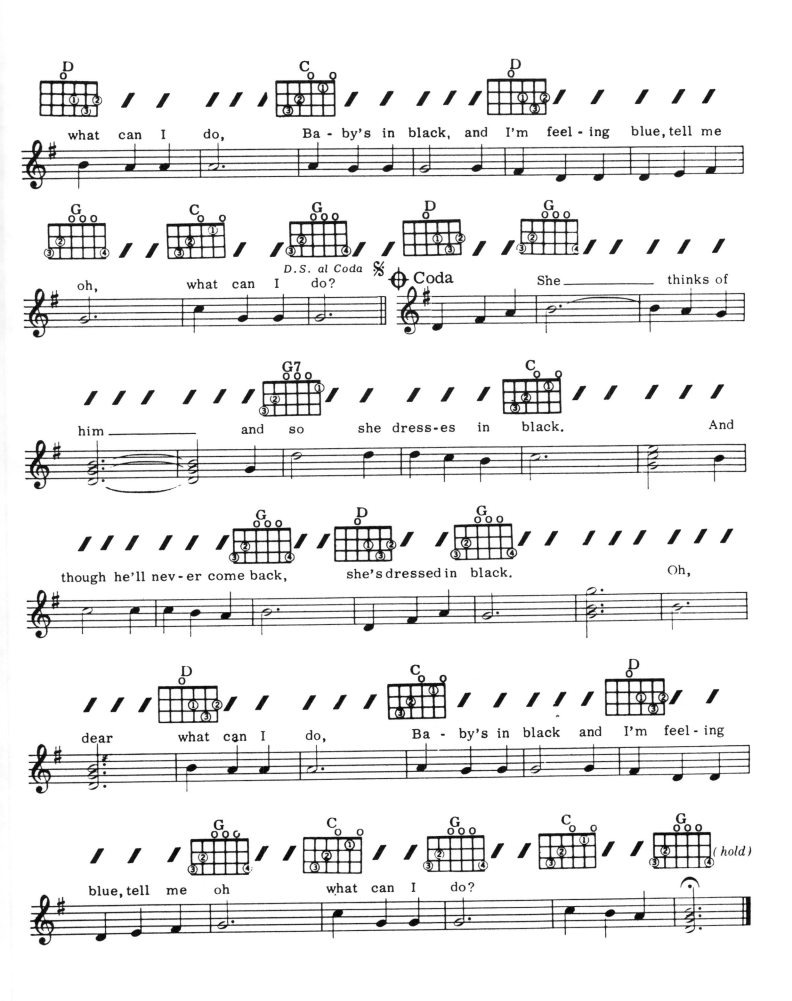

BACK IN THE U.S.S.R.

By JOHN LENNON and PAUL McCARTNEY

Starting note
for singing:

Moderately

THE BALLAD OF JOHN AND YOKO

By JOHN LENNON and PAUL McCARTNEY

Bridge

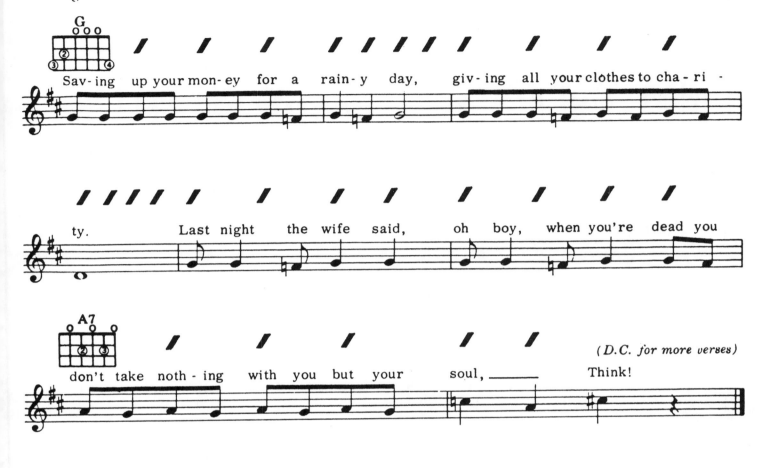

Sav-ing up your mon-ey for a rain-y day, giv-ing all your clothes to cha-ri-ty.

Last night the wife said, oh boy, when you're dead you don't take noth-ing with you but your soul, _____ Think!

(D.C. for more verses)

Additional Verses

2. Finally made the plane into Paris, honeymooning down the Seine,
   Peter Brown called to say, you can make it O.K.,
   You can get married in Gibraltar near Spain.
   Christ! You know it ain't easy, you know how hard it can be.
   The way things are going, they're going to crucify me.

3. Drove from Paris to the Amsterdam Hilton, talking in our beds for a week.
   The newspapers said, say what're you doing in bed,
   I said we're only trying to get us some peace. Christ! You know it ain't easy (etc.)

(Go to bridge)

4. Made a lightning trip to Vienna, eating choc'late cake in a bag.
   The newspapers said, she's gone to his head, they look just like two Gurus in drag.
   Christ, you know it ain't easy (etc.)

5. Caught the early plane back to London, fifty acorns tied in a sack.
   The men from the press said we wish you success, it's good to have the both of you back.
   Christ, you know it ain't easy (etc.)

Because

By JOHN LENNON and PAUL McCARTNEY

BIRTHDAY

By JOHN LENNON and PAUL McCARTNEY

BLACKBIRD

By JOHN LENNON and PAUL McCARTNEY

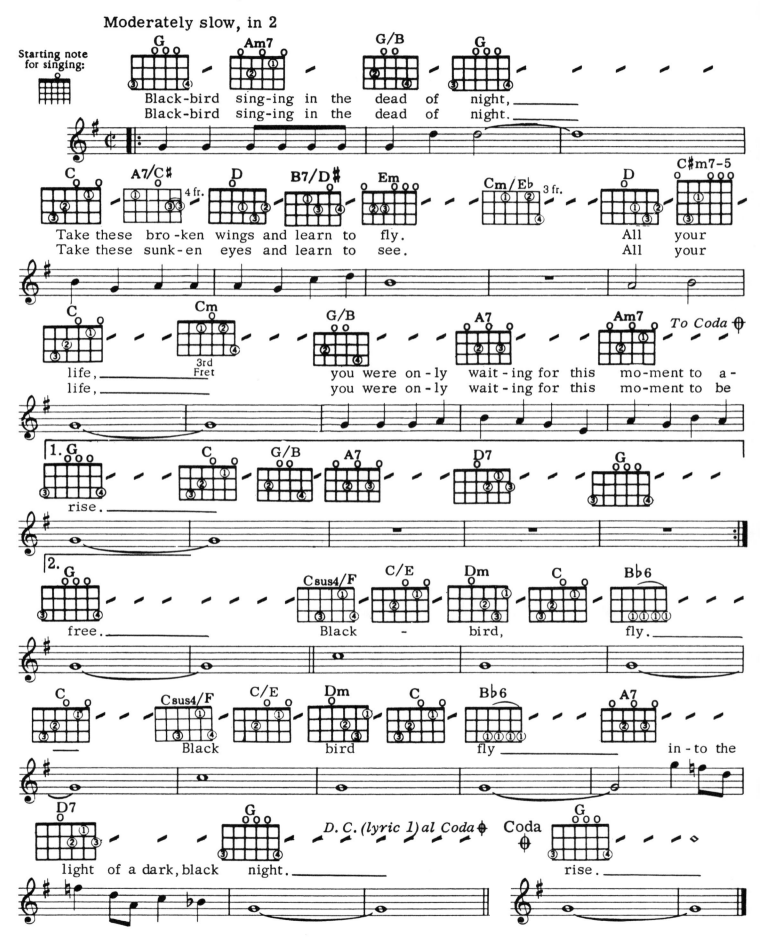

Moderately slow, in 2

Starting note for singing:

Black-bird sing-ing in the dead of night,
Black-bird sing-ing in the dead of night.

Take these bro-ken wings and learn to fly. All your
Take these sunk-en eyes and learn to see. All your

life, you were on-ly wait-ing for this mo-ment to a-
life, you were on-ly wait-ing for this mo-ment to be

To Coda

1. rise.

2. free. Black - bird, fly.

Black bird fly in-to the

light of a dark, black night.

D.C. (lyric 1) al Coda Coda rise.

BLUE JAY WAY

By GEORGE HARRISON

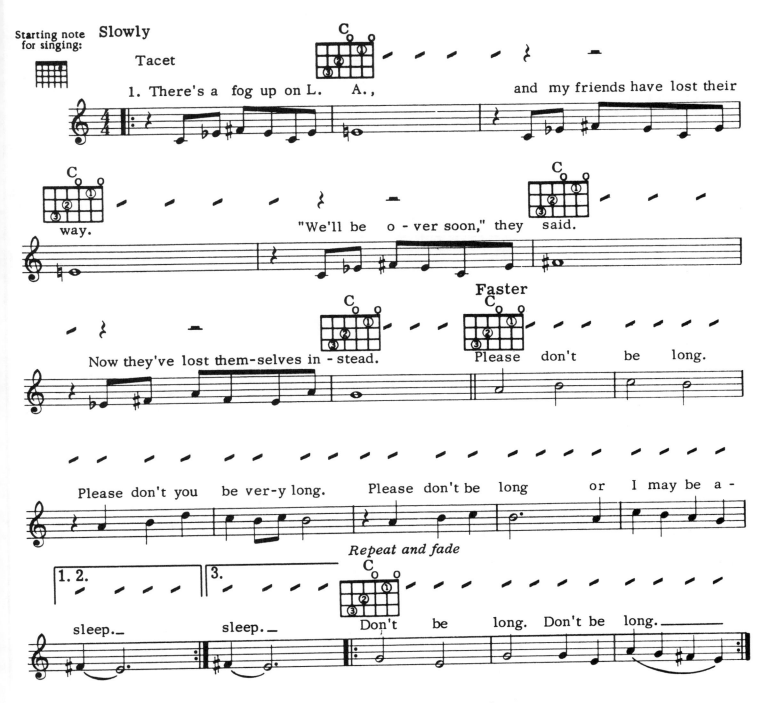

2. Well, it only goes to show, and I told them where to go.
   Ask a policeman on the street; There's so many there to meet.
   Please don't be long. *(etc.)*

3. Now it's past my bed I know, and I'd really like to go.
   Soon will be the break of day, sitting here in Blue Jay Way.
   Please don't be long. *(etc.)*

CAN'T BUY ME LOVE

By JOHN LENNON and PAUL McCARTNEY

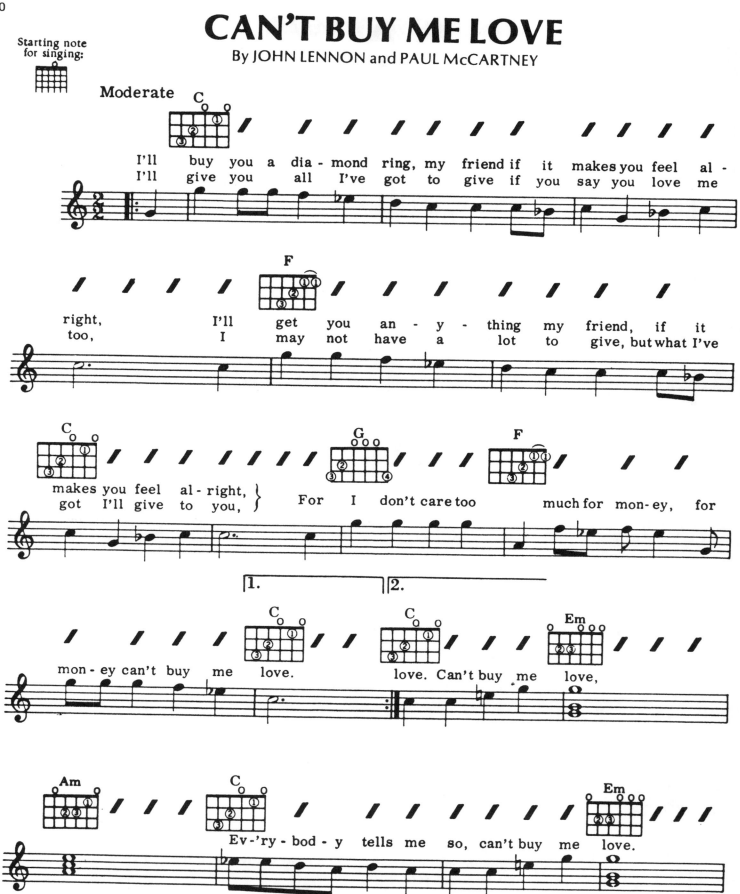

CARRY THAT WEIGHT

By JOHN LENNON and PAUL McCARTNEY

Starting note
for singing:

Moderato

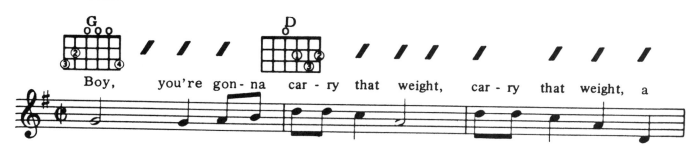

Boy, you're gon-na car-ry that weight, car-ry that weight, a

long time. Boy, you're gon-na car-ry that weight,

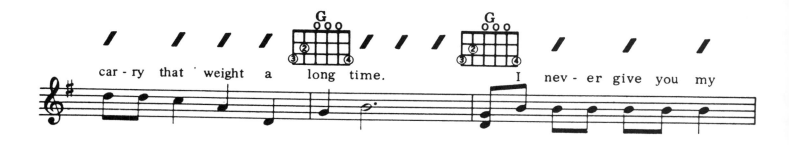

car-ry that weight a long time. I nev-er give you my

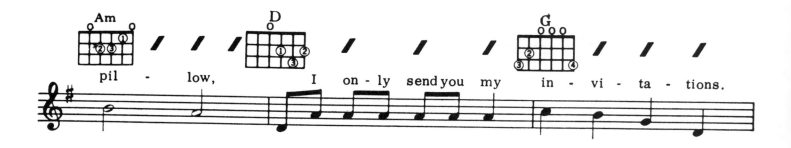

pil - low, I on-ly send you my in-vi-ta-tions.

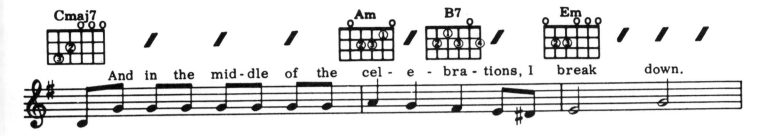

And in the mid-dle of the cel - e - bra - tions, I break down.

Boy, you're gon - na car - ry that weight,

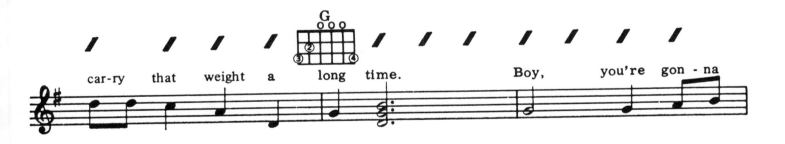

car-ry that weight a long time. Boy, you're gon - na

car-ry that weight, car - ry that weight a long time.

Starting note
for singing:

COME TOGETHER

By JOHN LENNON and PAUL McCARTNEY

Moderately

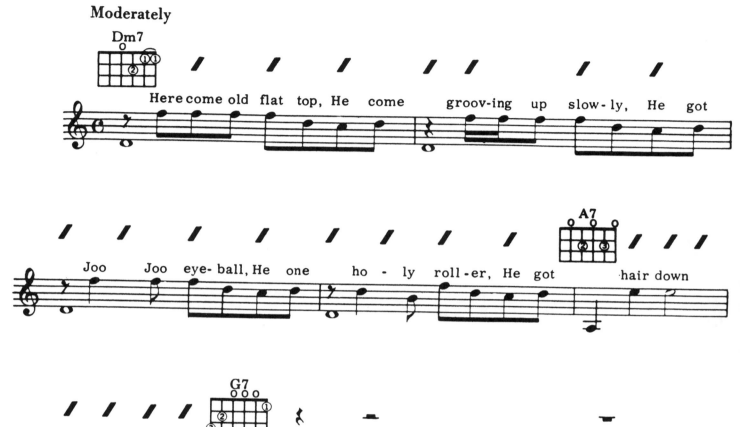

Here come old flat top, He come grooving up slow-ly, He got

Joo Joo eye-ball, He one ho-ly roll-er, He got hair down

to his knee; Got to be a jo-ker, he just do what he please.

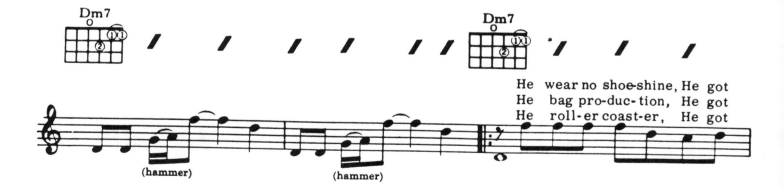

(hammer)   (hammer)

He wear no shoe-shine, He got
He bag pro-duc-tion, He got
He roll-er coast-er, He got

THE CONTINUING STORY OF BUNGALOW BILL

By JOHN LENNON and PAUL McCARTNEY

Starting note for singing:

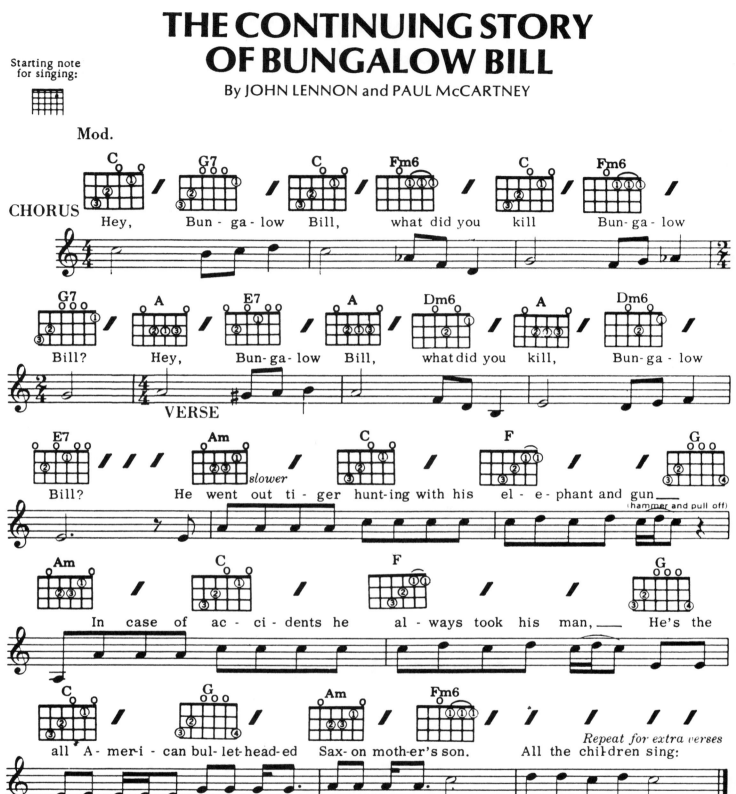

2. Deep in the jungle where the mighty tiger lies
   Bill and his elephants were taken by surprise,
   So Captain Marvel zapped him right between the eyes.   All the children sing: (*Chorus*)

3. The children asked him if to kill was not a sin,
   "Not when he looked so fierce," his mother butted in,
   If looks could kill it would have been us instead of him.   All the children sing: (*Chorus*)

A DAY IN THE LIFE

By JOHN LENNON and PAUL McCARTNEY

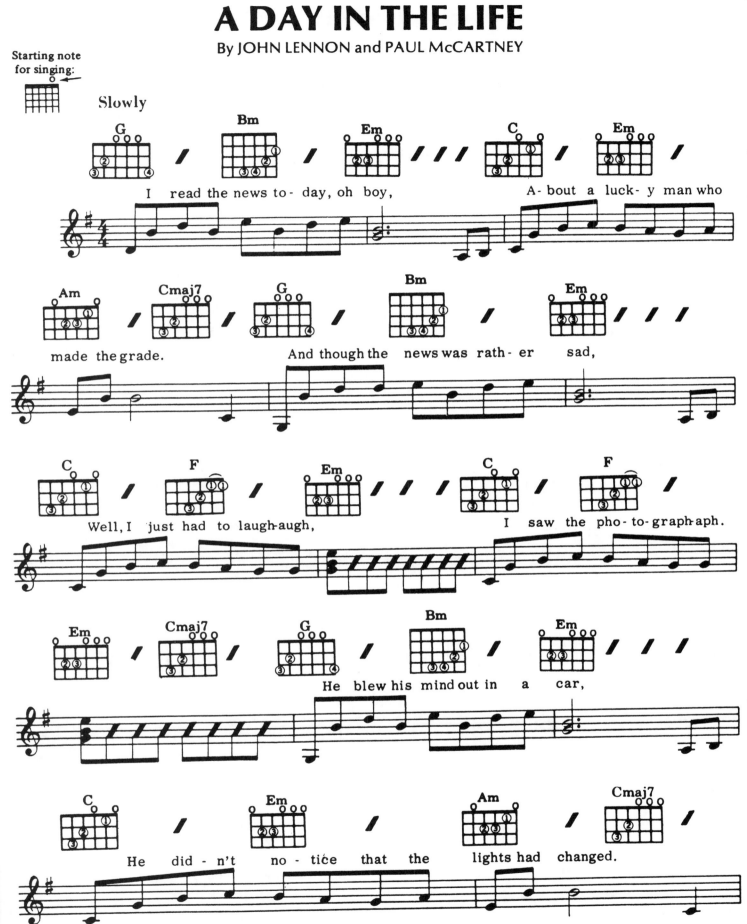

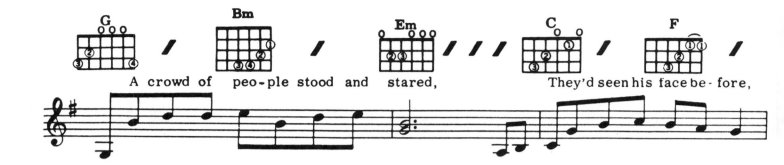

A crowd of peo-ple stood and stared, They'd seen his face be-fore,

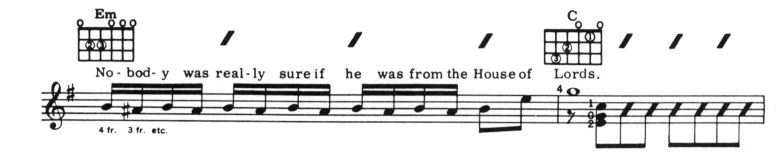

No-bod-y was real-ly sure if he was from the House of Lords.

4 fr.   3 fr. etc.

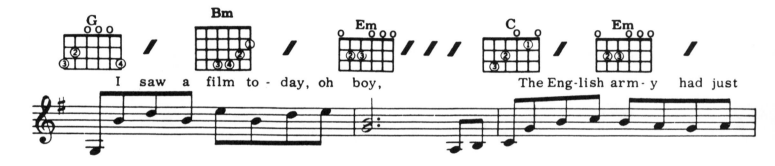

I saw a film to-day, oh boy, The Eng-lish arm-y had just

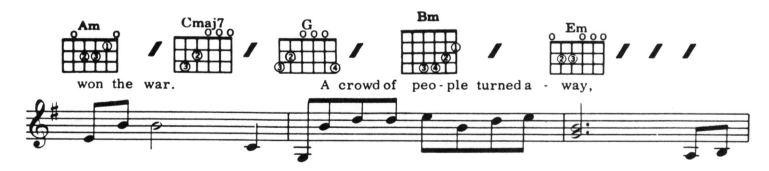

won the war. A crowd of peo-ple turned a-way,

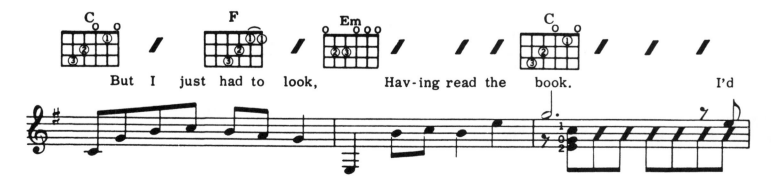

But I just had to look, Hav-ing read the book. I'd

Bm G Am7 Em No chords
love to turn you on.
G Bm Em C Em
I heard the news to-day, oh boy, Four thou-sand holes in Black-burn
Am Cmaj7 G Bm Em
Lan-ca-shire. And though the holes were ra-ther small,
C F Em
They had to count them all, Now they know how man-y holes it takes to fill the Al-bert
C Bm G Am7 E (hold)
Hall. I'd love to turn you on.

CRY BABY CRY

By JOHN LENNON and PAUL McCARTNEY

Slowly, in 2

Cry, _____ ba - by, cry; _____ make your moth - er sigh. She's old e - nough_ to know_ bet - ter. 1. The King of Mar - i - gold was in the kitch - en cook - ing break-fast for the queen._ The

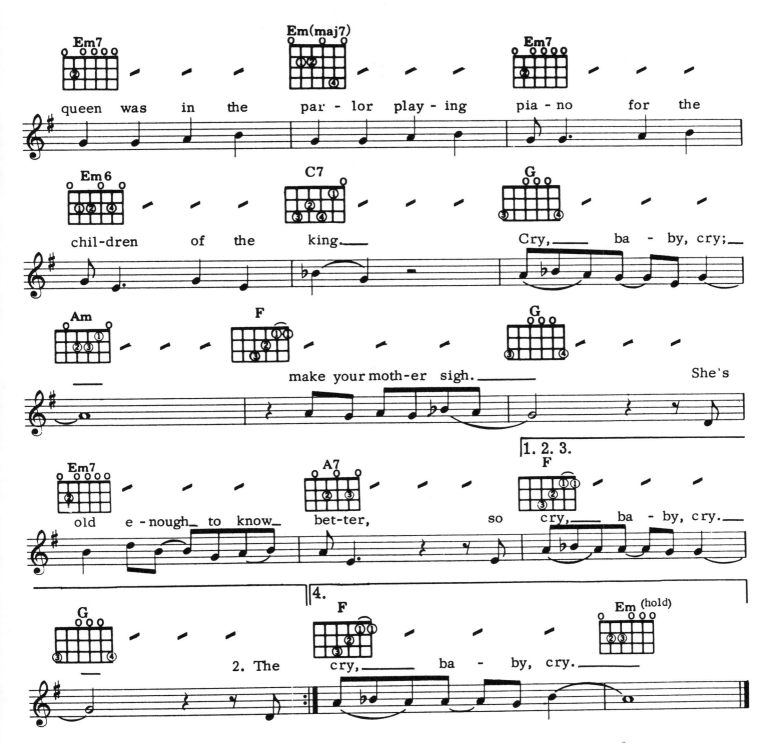

2. The king was in the garden picking flowers for a friend who came to play.
   The queen was in the playroom painting pictures for the children's holiday.
   Cry, baby, cry; *(etc.)*

3. The Duchess of Kircaldy always smiling and arriving late for tea.
   The duke was having problems with a message at the local Bird and Bee.
   Cry, baby, cry; *(etc.)*

4. At twelve o'clock a meeting 'round the table for a seance in the dark,
   With voices out of nowhere put on specially by the children for a lark.
   Cry, baby, cry; *(etc.)*

DAY TRIPPER

By JOHN LENNON and PAUL McCARTNEY

DEAR PRUDENCE

By JOHN LENNON and PAUL McCARTNEY

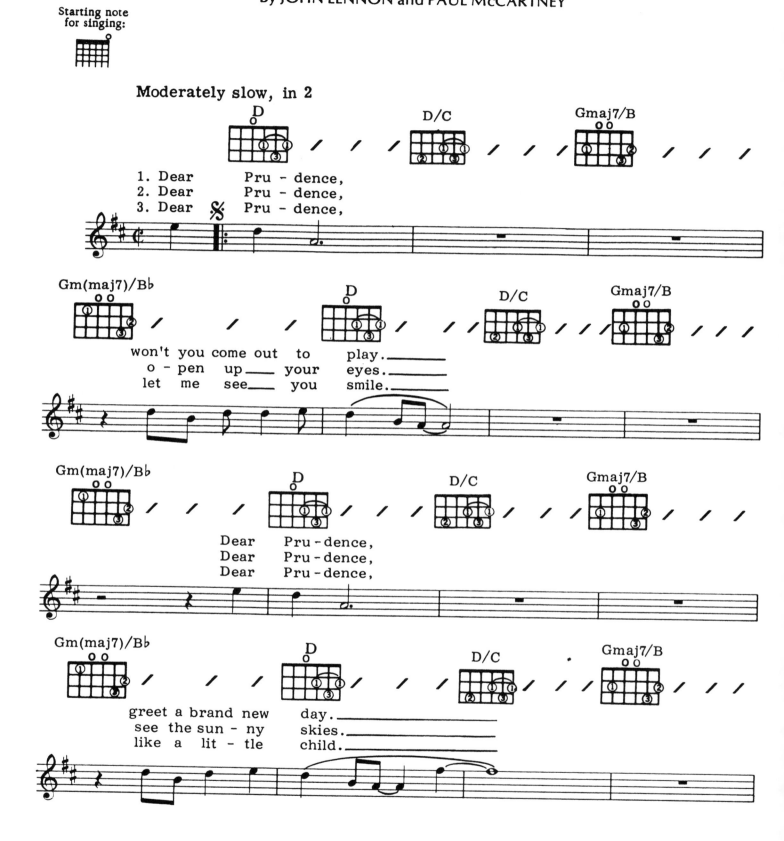

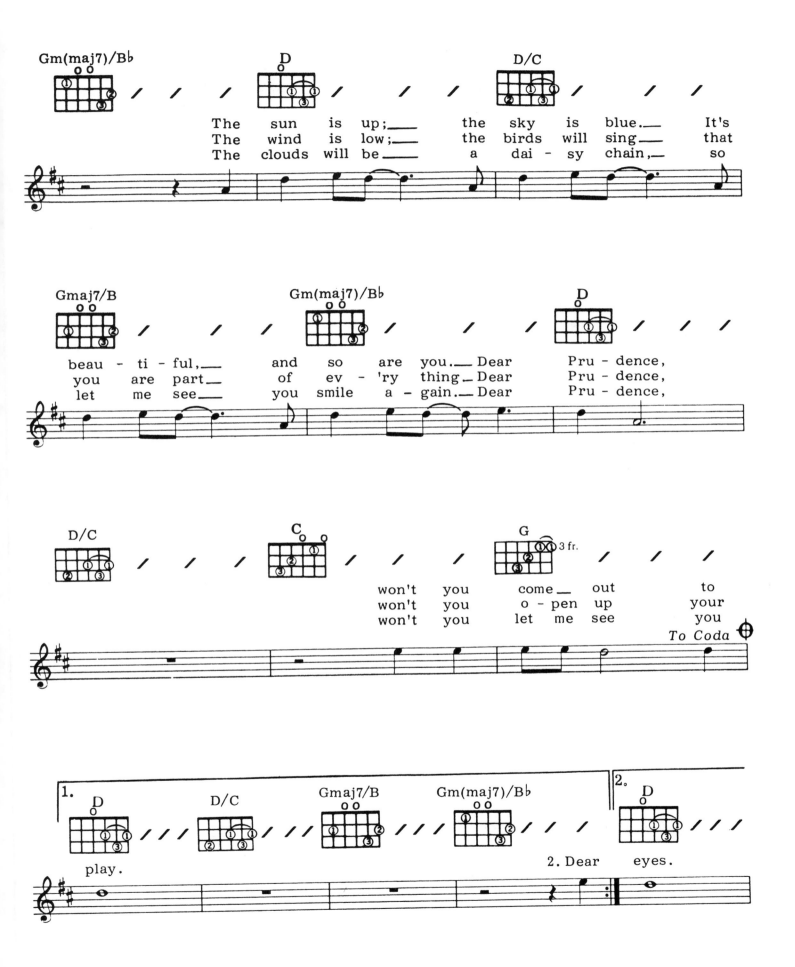

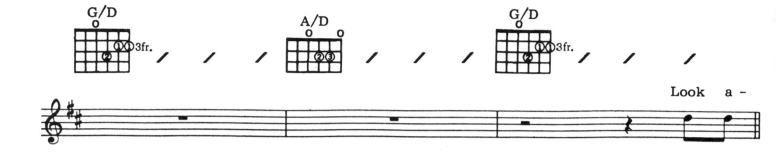

Look a-

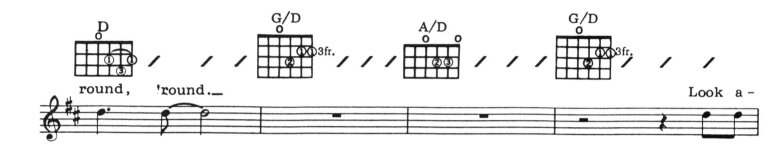

round, 'round.—

Look a-

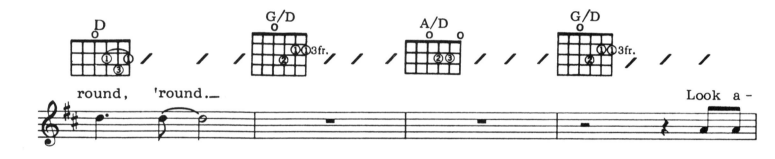

round, 'round.—

Look a-

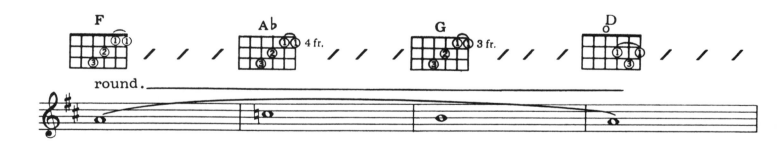

round._____

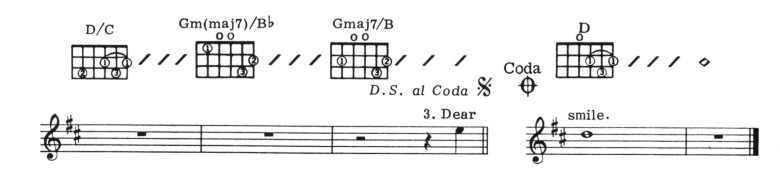

D.S. al Coda 𝄋

Coda 𝄌

3. Dear

smile.

DIG IT

By JOHN LENNON, PAUL McCARTNEY, GEORGE HARRISON and RICHARD STARKEY

Starting note
for singing:

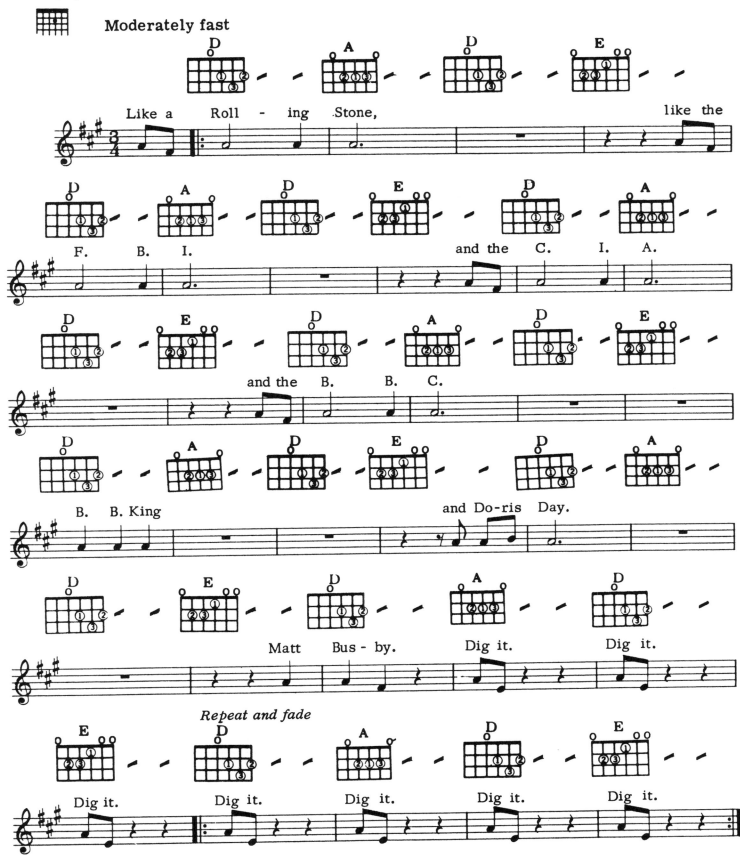

DON'T LET ME DOWN

By JOHN LENNON and PAUL McCARTNEY

DR. ROBERT

By JOHN LENNON and PAUL McCARTNEY

Starting note
for singing:

Moderately, in 2

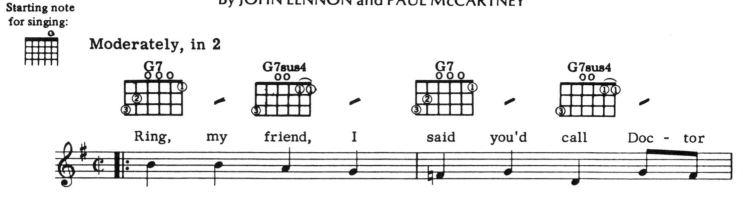

Ring, my friend, I said you'd call Doc-tor

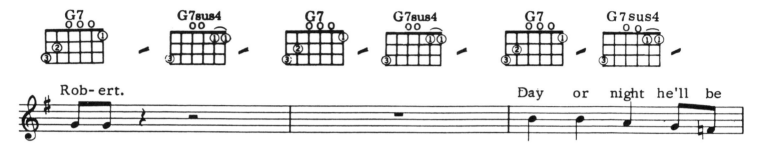

Rob-ert. Day or night he'll be

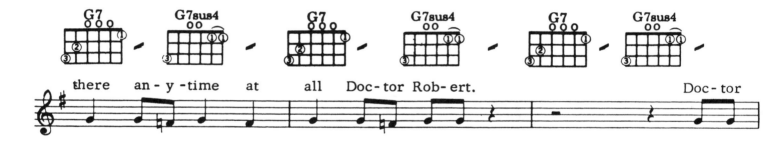

there an-y-time at all Doc-tor Rob-ert. Doc-tor

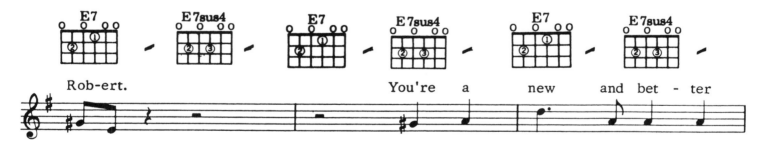

Rob-ert. You're a new and bet-ter

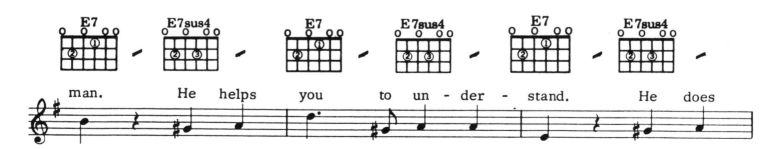

man. He helps you to un-der-stand. He does

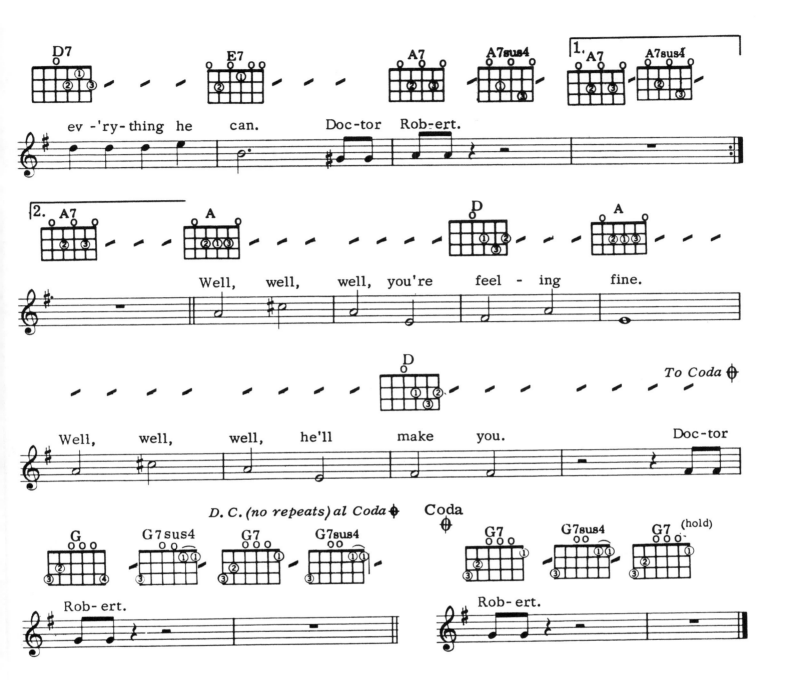

2. If you're down he'll pick you up, Dr. Robert.
   Take a drink from his special cup, Dr. Robert.
   Dr. Robert.
   He's a man you must believe, helping everyone in need.
   No one can succeed like Dr. Robert.
   Well, well, well, *(etc.)*

3. My friend works with the national health, Dr. Robert.
   Don't pay money just to see yourself with Dr. Robert.
   Dr. Robert.
   You're a new and better man. He helps you to understand.
   He does everything he can, Dr. Robert.
   Well, well, well, *(etc.)*

DRIVE MY CAR

By JOHN LENNON and PAUL McCARTNEY

Starting note for singing:

Medium Rock beat

1. Asked a girl what she want-ed to be.___

She said, "Ba-by, can't you see?___

I wan-na be fa-mous, a star of the screen,_ but

you can do some-thing in be - tween.___

Ba-by, you can drive my car.

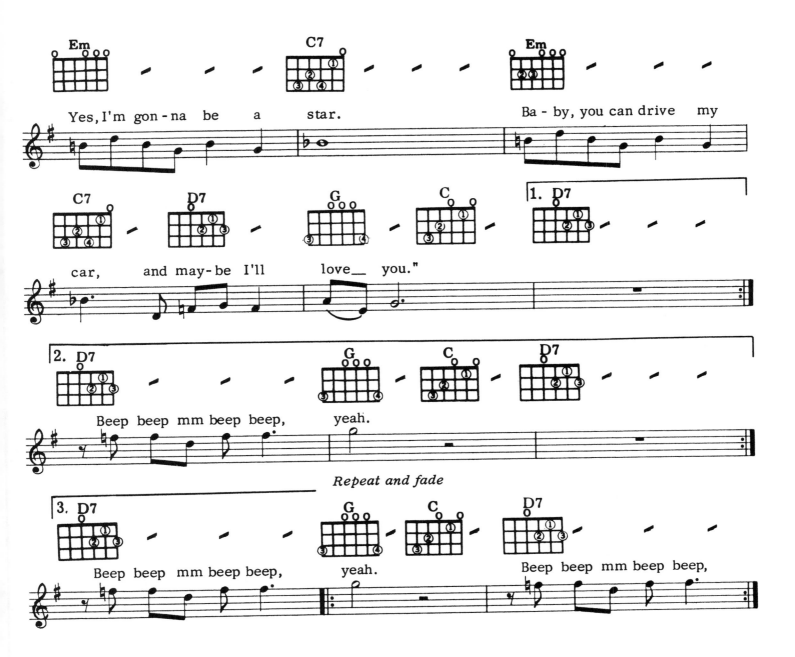

Yes, I'm gon-na be a star. Ba - by, you can drive my

car, and may-be I'll love__ you."

2. Beep beep mm beep beep, yeah.

Repeat and fade

3. Beep beep mm beep beep, yeah. Beep beep mm beep beep,

2. I told that girl that my prospects were good.
   She said, "Baby, it's understood.
   Working for peanuts is all very fine,
   But I can show you a better time.
   Baby, you can drive my car. *(etc.)*

3. I told that girl I could start right away.
   She said, "Baby, I've got something to say.
   I got no car and it's breaking my heart,
   But I've found a driver, that's a start.
   Baby, you can drive my car. *(etc.)*

EIGHT DAYS A WEEK

By JOHN LENNON and PAUL McCARTNEY

Starting note for
singing on guitar:

Moderato

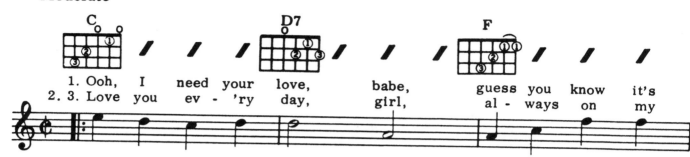

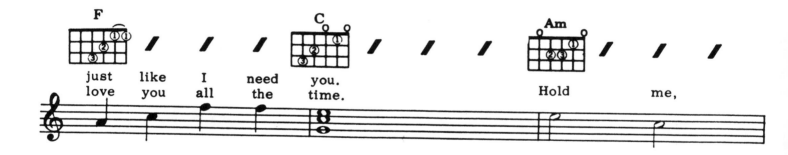

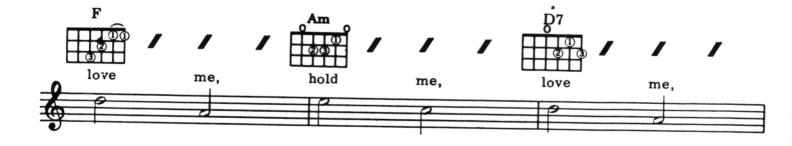

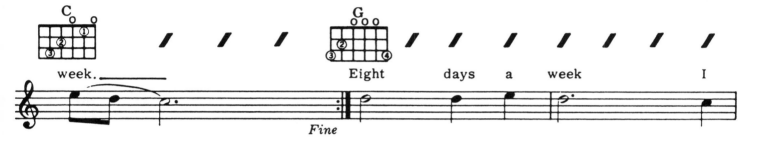

ELEANOR RIGBY

By JOHN LENNON and PAUL McCARTNEY

Starting note
for singing:

Ah   look at all the lone - ly peo - ple!

E - lea - nor Rig - by,   picks up the rice ___ in the church

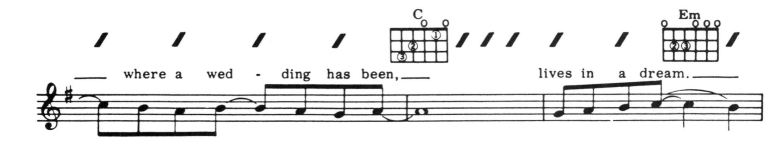

___ where a wed - ding has been, ___ lives in a dream. ___

Waits at the win - dow, wear-ing the face ___ that she keeps

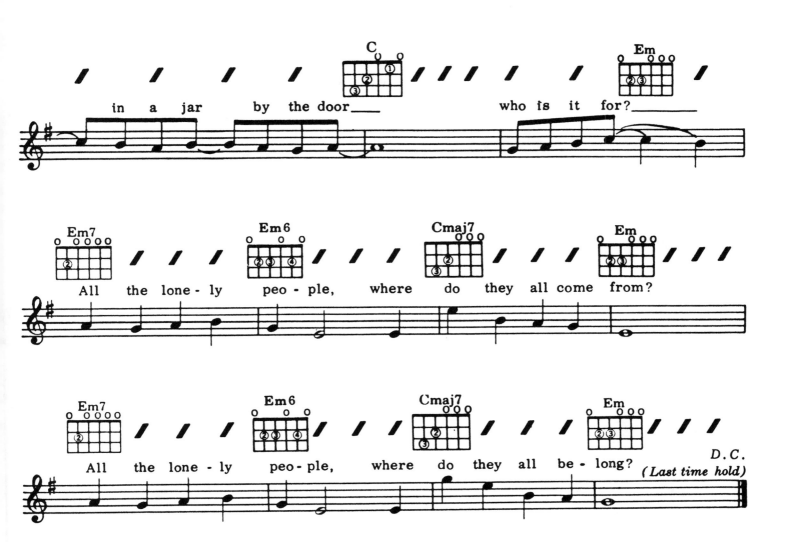

2. Father McKenzie, writing the words of a sermon that no one will hear, no one comes near.

   Look at him working, darning his socks in the night when there's nobody there, what does he care?

   All the lonely people, where do they all come from?

   All the lonely people, where do they all belong?

3. Eleanor Rigby, died in the church and was buried along with her name, nobody came.

   Father McKenzie, wiping the dirt from his hands as he walks from the grave, no one was saved.

   All the lonely people, where do they all come from?

   All the lonely people, where do they all belong?

THE END

By JOHN LENNON and PAUL McCARTNEY

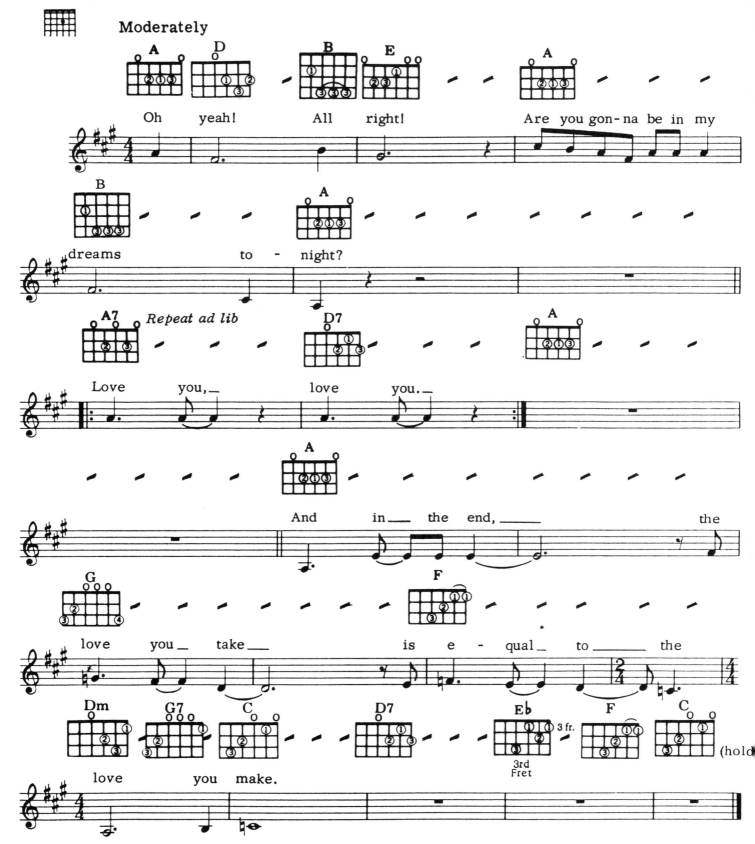

GET BACK

By JOHN LENNON and PAUL McCARTNEY

Sweet Loretta Modern thought she was a woman,
But she was another man.
All the girls around her said she's got it coming,
But she gets it while she can.

Get back! Get back!
Get back to where you once belonged.
Get back! Get back!
Get back to where you once belonged.

EVERY LITTLE THING

By JOHN LENNON and PAUL McCARTNEY

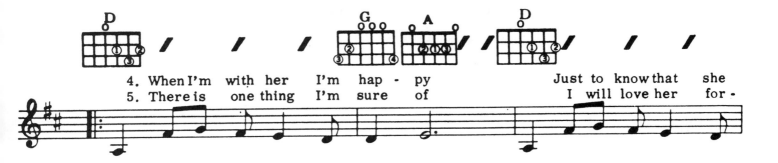

4. When I'm with her I'm hap - py Just to know that she
5. There is one thing I'm sure of I will love her for -

loves __ me Yes, I know that she loves me now.
ev - er For I know love will nev - er die.

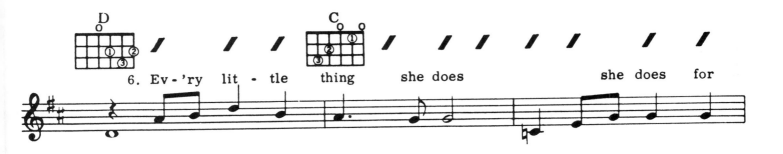

6. Ev - 'ry lit - tle thing she does she does for

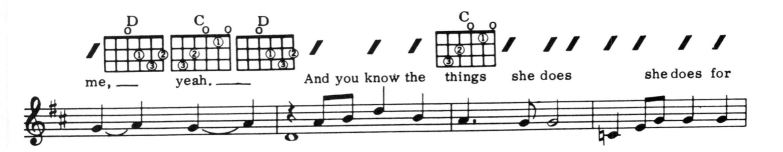

me, __ yeah. __ And you know the things she does she does for

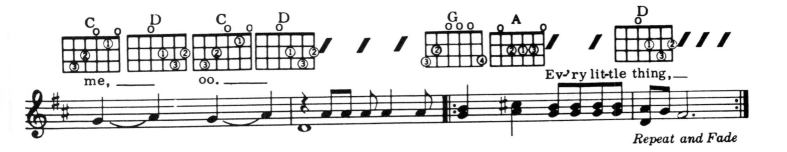

me, __ oo. __ Ev - ry lit - tle thing, __

Repeat and Fade

EVERYBODY'S GOT SOMETHING TO HIDE EXCEPT ME AND MY MONKEY

By JOHN LENNON and PAUL McCARTNEY

FIXING A HOLE

By JOHN LENNON and PAUL McCARTNEY

THE FOOL ON THE HILL

By JOHN LENNON and PAUL McCARTNEY

Starting note
for singing:

Fairly bright

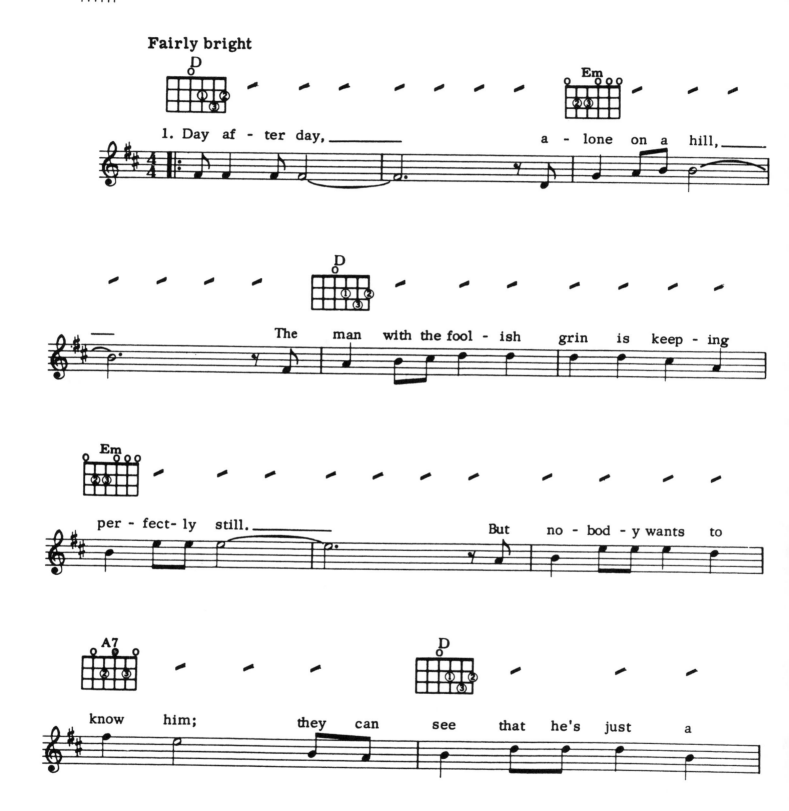

1. Day af - ter day, _____ a - lone on a hill, _____

The man with the fool - ish grin is keep - ing

per - fect - ly still. _____ But no - bod - y wants to

know him; they can see that he's just a

2. Well on the way, head in a cloud,
   The man of a thousand voices talking perfectly loud.
   But nobody ever hears him or the sound he appears to make.
   And he never seems to notice.
   But the fool on the hill *(etc.)*

3. *Instrumental* _____

   Nobody seems to like him; they can tell what he wants to do.
   And he never shows his feelings.
   But the fool on the hill *(etc.)*

4. *Instrumental* _____

   He never listens to them, he knows that they're the fools,
   They don't like him,
   But the fool on the hill *(etc.)*

FOR NO ONE

By JOHN LENNON and PAUL McCARTNEY

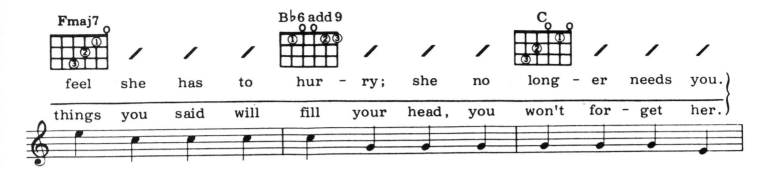

feel she has to hur - ry; she no long - er needs you.
things you said will fill your head, you won't for - get her.

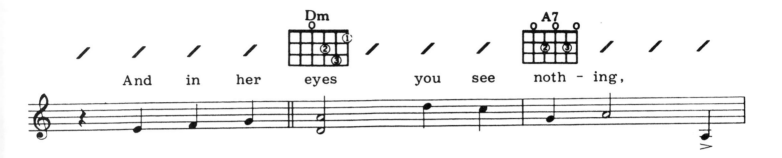

And in her eyes you see noth - ing,

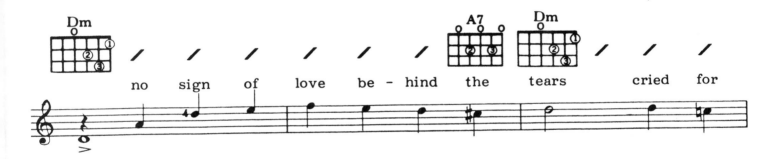

no sign of love be - hind the tears cried for

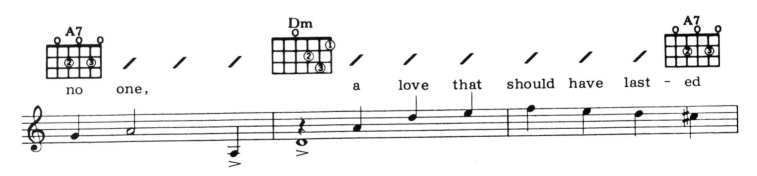

no one, a love that should have last - ed

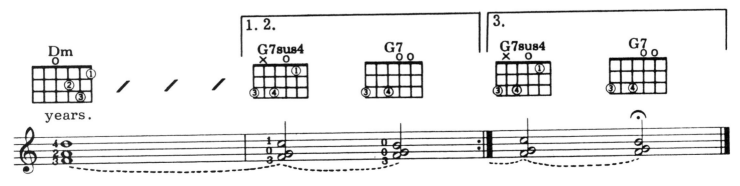

years.

GETTING BETTER

By JOHN LENNON and PAUL McCARTNEY

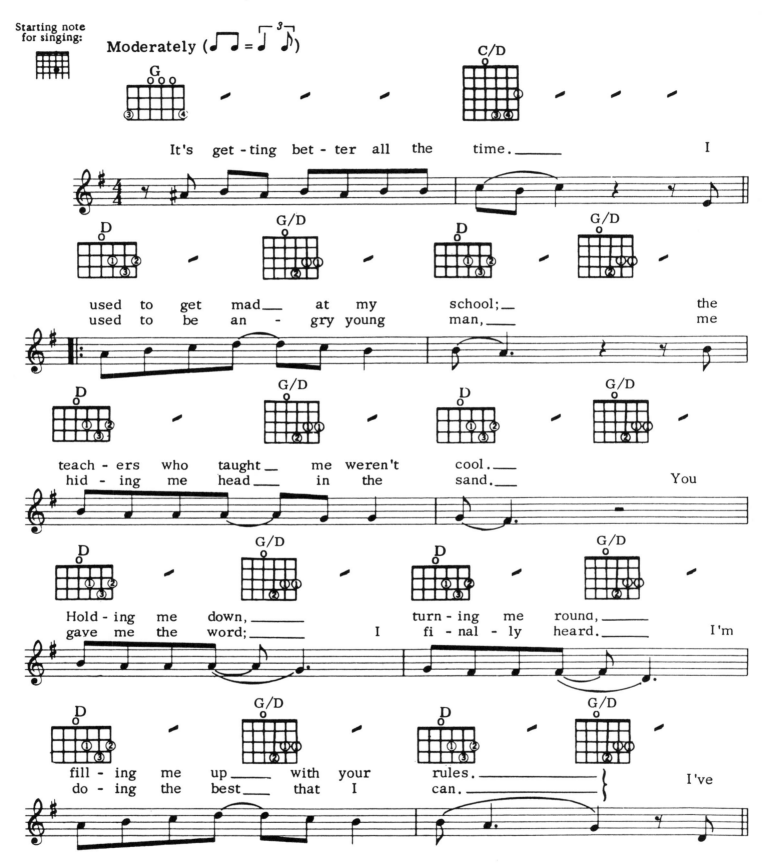

It's get-ting bet-ter all the time.____ I

used to get mad____ at my school;____ the
used to be an-gry young man,____ me

teach-ers who taught____ me weren't cool.____ You
hid-ing me head____ in the sand.____

Hold-ing me down,____ turn-ing me round,____ I'm
gave me the word;____ I fi-nal-ly heard.____

fill-ing me up____ with your rules.____ I've
do-ing the best____ that I can.____

got to ad-mit___ it's get-ting bet-ter; a lit-tle bet-ter all the

time. I have to ad-mit___ it's get-ting bet-ter; it's get-ting

bet-ter since you've been mine. Me

Get-ting so much bet-ter all the time. It's get-ting bet-ter all the

time.___ Bet-ter, bet-ter, bet - ter.

It's get-ting bet-ter all the time._____

82

GLASS ONION

By JOHN LENNON and PAUL McCARTNEY

84

Oh, yeah,

Oh, yeah,   Oh,

yeah,

Look - ing through a glass on - ion.

D.C. al Fine

N.C.

85

GIRL

By JOHN LENNON and PAUL McCARTNEY

Starting note
for singing:

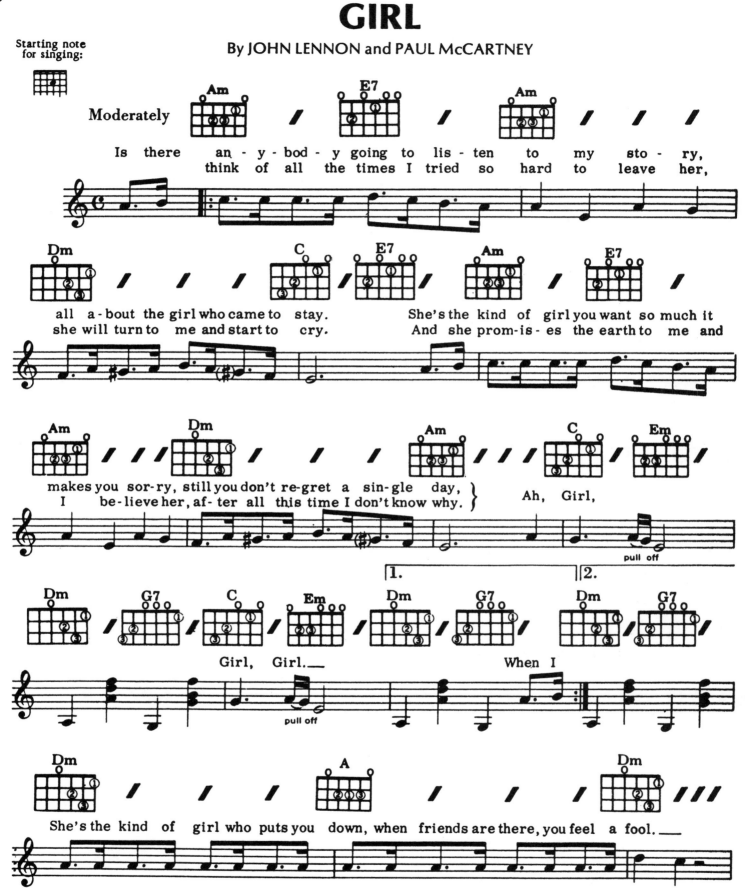

Moderately

Is there an-y-bod-y going to lis-ten to my sto-ry,
think of all the times I tried so hard to leave her,

all a-bout the girl who came to stay.
she will turn to me and start to cry.
She's the kind of girl you want so much it
And she prom-is-es the earth to me and

makes you sor-ry, still you don't re-gret a sin-gle day,
I be-lieve her, af-ter all this time I don't know why.
Ah, Girl,

1.
Girl, Girl.___
2.
When I

pull off

pull off

She's the kind of girl who puts you down, when friends are there, you feel a fool.___

87

GIVE PEACE A CHANCE

By JOHN LENNON and PAUL McCARTNEY

(Strike fingerboard or body of the guitar)

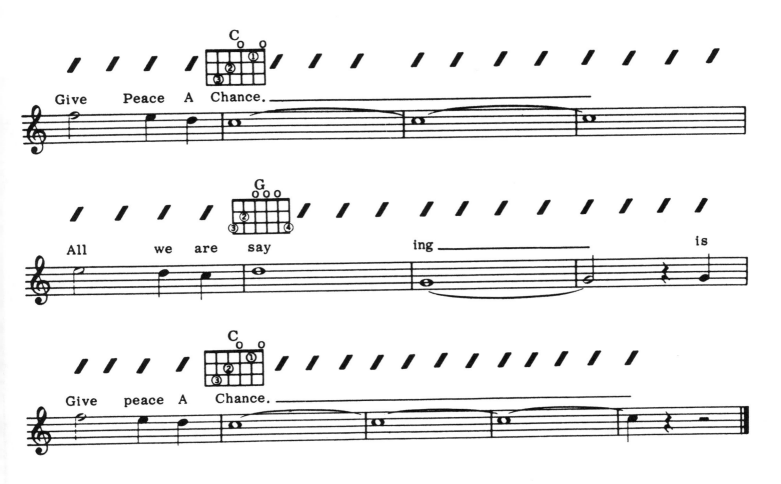

2. Ev'rybody's talking about
   Ministers, Sinisters, Banisters and Canisters,
   Bishops and Fishops, Rabbits and Popeyes,
   Bye-bye Bye-byes.

   All we are saying is Give Peace A Chance.
   All we are saying is Give Peace A Chance.

3. Let me tell you now,
   Ev'rybody's talking about
   Revolution, Evolution, Mastication, Flagellation,
   Regulations, Integregations, Meditation, United Nations,
   Congratulations.

   All we are saying is Give Peace A Chance.
   All we are saying is Give Peace A Chance.

4. Oh, let's stick to it,
   Ev'rybody's talking about
   John and Yoko, Timmy Leary, Rosemary, Tommy Smothers,
   Bobby Dylan, Tommy Cooper, Derek Taylor, Norman Mailer,
   Alan Ginsberg, Hare Krishna, Hare, Hare Krishna.

   All we are saying is Give Peace A Chance.
   All we are saying is Give Peace A Chance.
   All we are saying is Give Peace A Chance.
   All we are saying is Give Peace A Chance.

GOLDEN SLUMBERS

By JOHN LENNON and PAUL McCARTNEY

Good Morning Good Morning

By JOHN LENNON and PAUL McCARTNEY

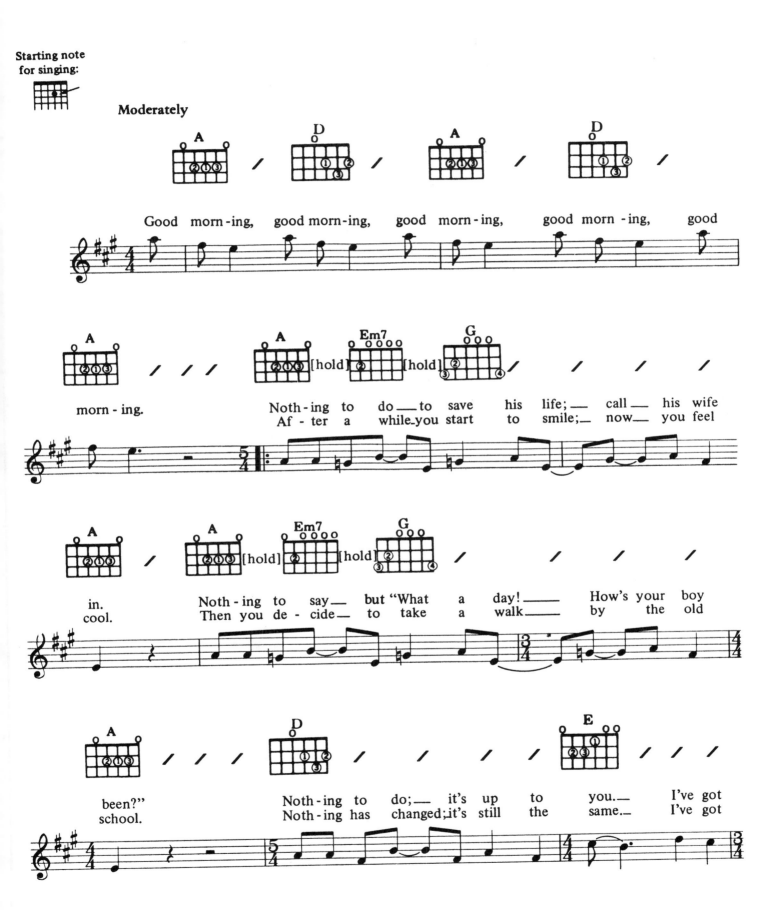

93

Good Day Sunshine

By JOHN LENNON and PAUL McCARTNEY

Starting note
for singing:

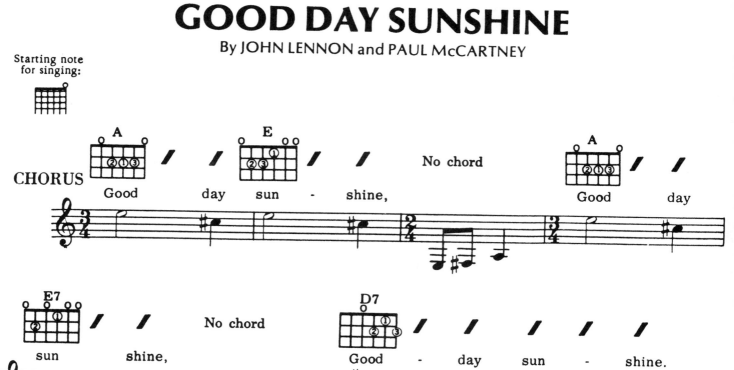

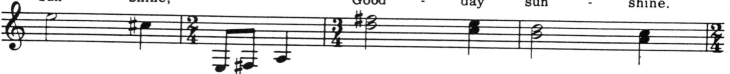

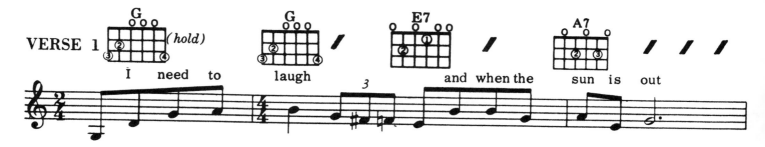

Repeat Chorus

VERSE 2

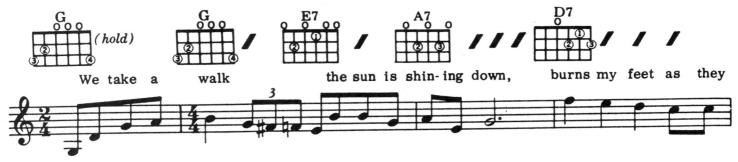

We take a walk the sun is shin-ing down, burns my feet as they

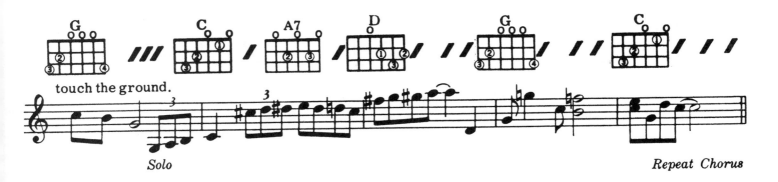

touch the ground.

Solo

Repeat Chorus

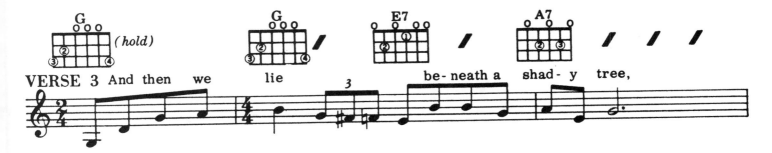

VERSE 3 And then we lie be-neath a shad-y tree,

I love her and she lov-ing me.____ She feels good she knows she's

look-ing fine, I'm so proud to know that she is mine.

Repeat Chorus and fade

GOOD NIGHT

By JOHN LENNON and PAUL McCARTNEY

Starting note for singing:

Slowly and dreamily

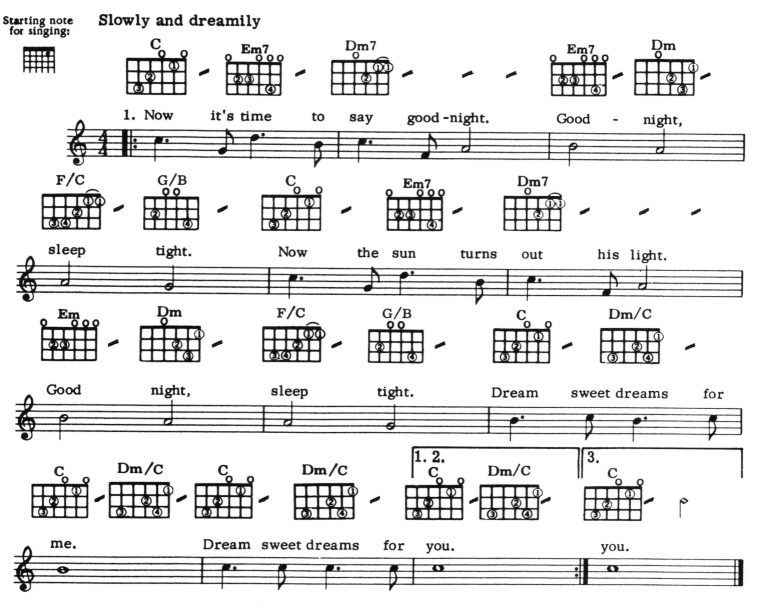

2. Close your eyes and I'll close mine.
   Goodnight, sleep tight.
   Now the moon begins to shine.
   Goodnight, sleep tight.
   Dream sweet dreams for me.
   Dream sweet dreams for you.

3. Close your eyes and I'll close mine.
   Goodnight, sleep tight.
   Now the sun turns out his light.
   Goodnight, sleep tight.
   Dream sweet dreams for me.
   Dream sweet dreams for you.

HAPPINESS IS A WARM GUN

By JOHN LENNON and PAUL McCARTNEY

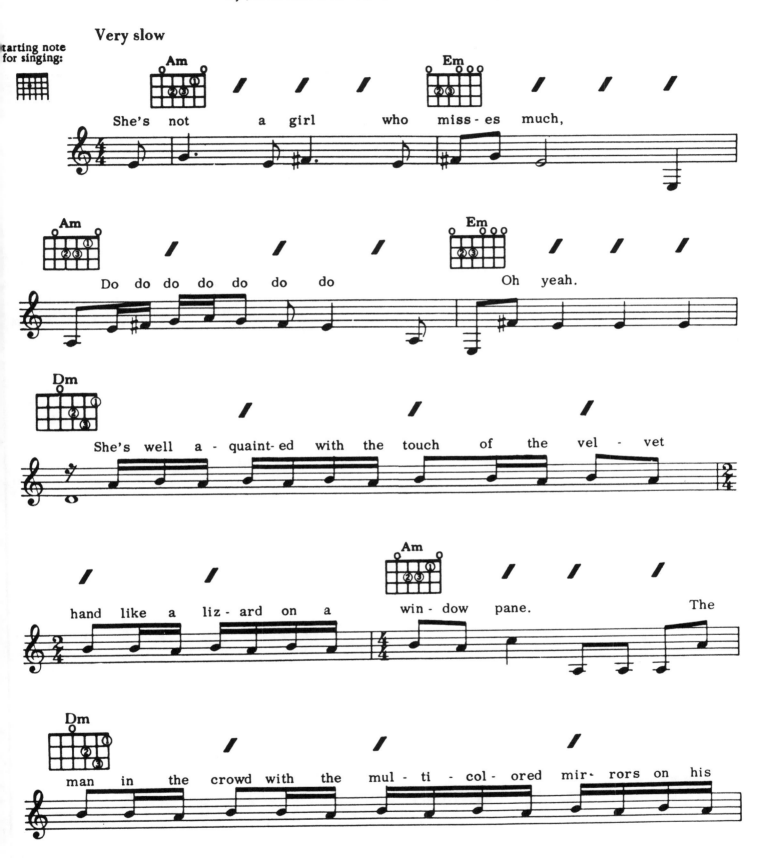

GOT TO GET YOU INTO MY LIFE

By JOHN LENNON and PAUL McCARTNEY

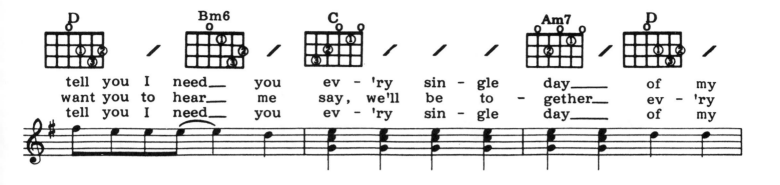

tell you I need___ you ev - 'ry sin - gle day_____ of my
want you to hear___ me say, we'll be to - gether___ ev - 'ry
tell you I need___ you ev - 'ry sin - gle day_____ of my

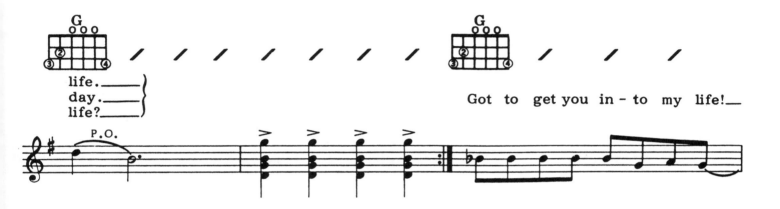

life._____
day._____
life?_____

Got to get you in - to my life!__

To Coda

D7sus4   N.C.

D.C. al Coda

Coda   G (hold)

A HARD DAY'S NIGHT

By JOHN LENNON and PAUL McCARTNEY

103

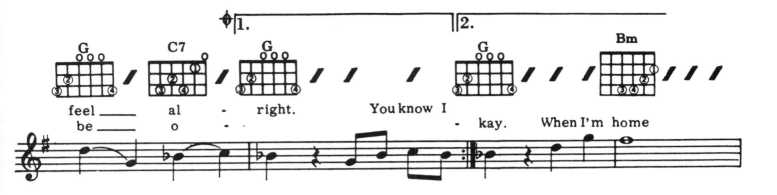

feel ____ al - right.   You know I
be ____ o - ___ - kay.   When I'm home

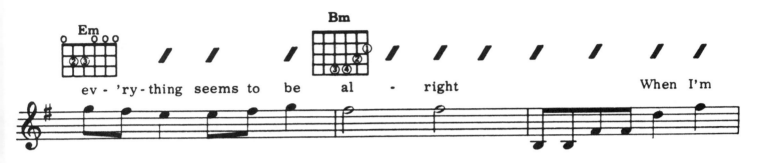

ev - 'ry-thing seems to be al - right   When I'm

home   feel-ing you hold-ing me tight   tight,   Yeah,

D.C. al ⊕ Coda
(use 1st verse)

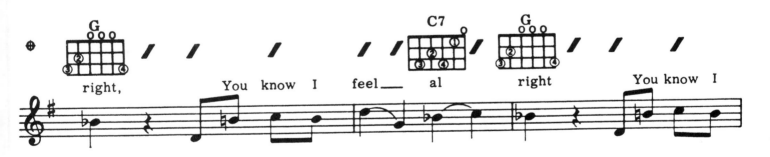

right,   You know I feel ___ al   right   You know I

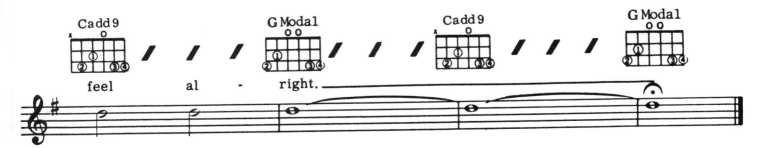

feel   al - right. _____

HELLO, GOODBYE

By JOHN LENNON and PAUL McCARTNEY

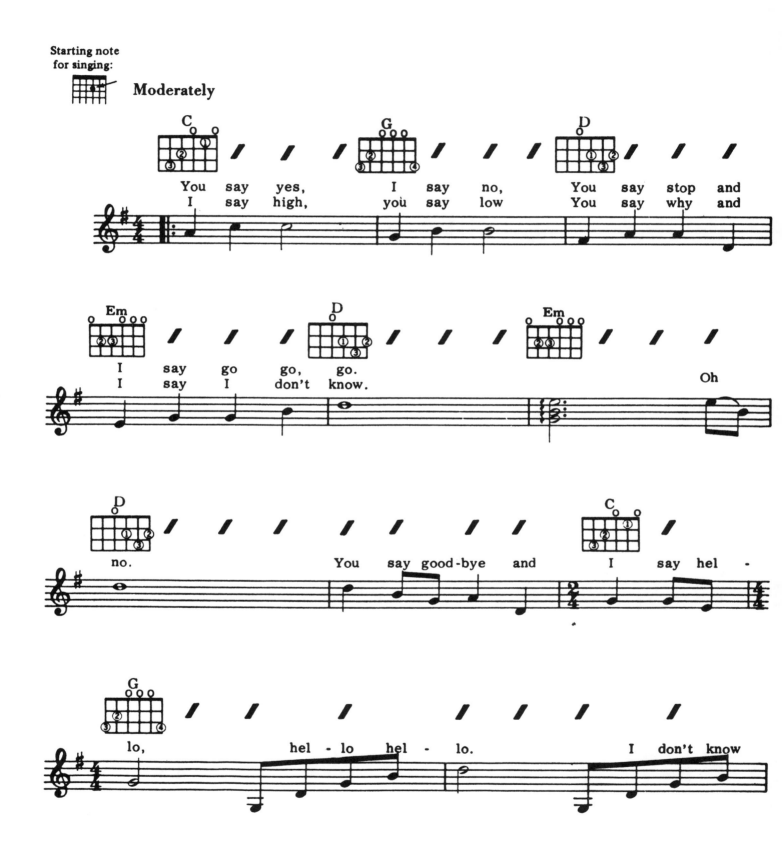

why you say good-bye, I say hel - lo, hel - lo, hel -

1.

lo. I don't know why you say good-bye, I say hel - lo.

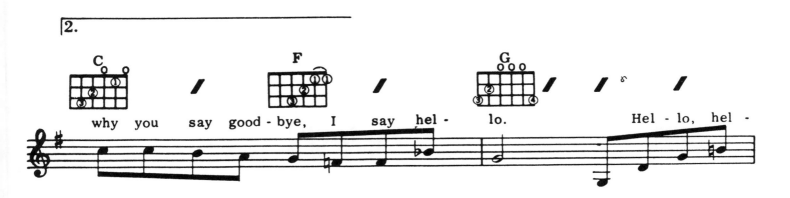

2.

why you say good - bye, I say hel - lo. Hel - lo, hel -

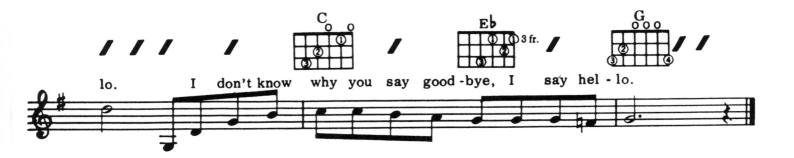

lo. I don't know why you say good - bye, I say hel - lo.

HELP!

By JOHN LENNON and PAUL McCARTNEY

107

HELTER SKELTER

By JOHN LENNON and PAUL McCARTNEY

2. Well will you, won't you want me to make you?
   I'm coming down fast but don't let me break you.
   Tell me, tell me, tell me the answer:
   You may be a lover but you ain't no dancer.
   Helter skelter etc.

3. Well do you, don't you want me to make you?
   I'm coming down fast but don't let me break you.
   Tell me, tell me, tell me the answer:
   You may be a lover but you ain't no dancer.
   Helter skelter etc.

HER MAJESTY

By JOHN LENNON and PAUL McCARTNEY

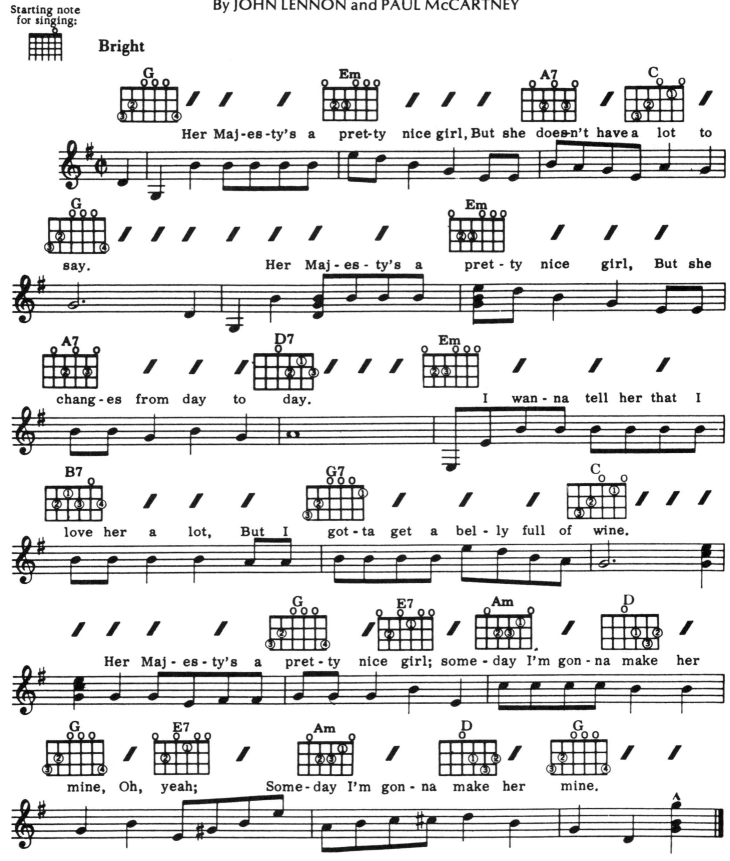

HONEY PIE

By JOHN LENNON and PAUL McCARTNEY

HERE THERE AND EVERYWHERE

By JOHN LENNON and PAUL McCARTNEY

Starting note
for singing:

Moderately slow

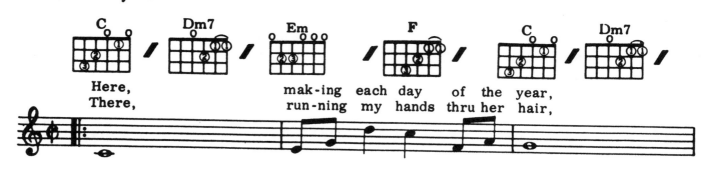

Here,
There,

mak-ing each day of the year,
run-ning my hands thru her hair,

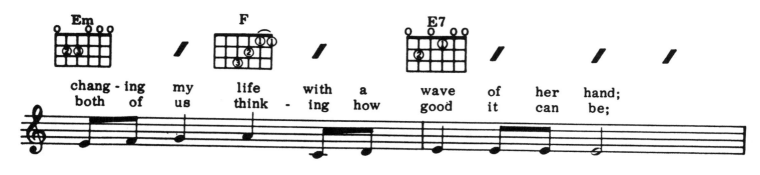

chang-ing my life with a wave of her hand;
both of us think - ing how good it can be;

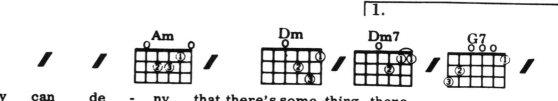

No-bod-y can de-ny that there's some-thing there.
Some-one is speak-ing but she does-n't know he's

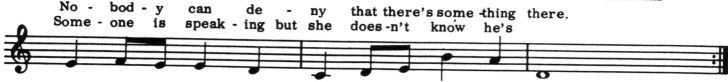

2.

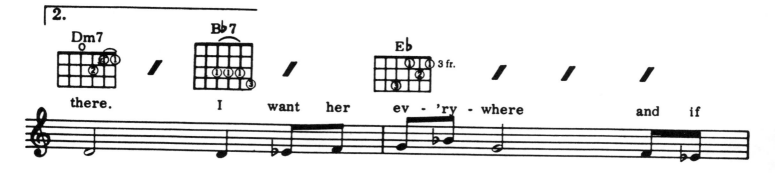

there. I want her ev-'ry-where and if

she's be - side me I know I need nev - er care...

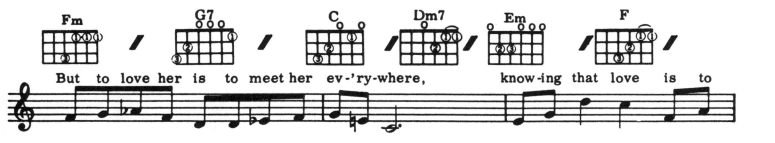

But to love her is to meet her ev -'ry-where, know-ing that love is to

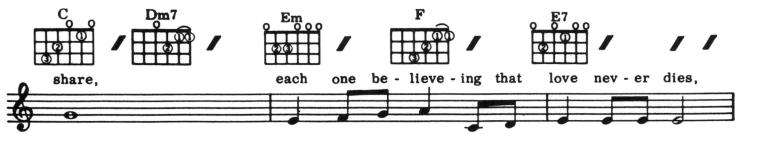

share, each one be - lieve - ing that love nev - er dies,

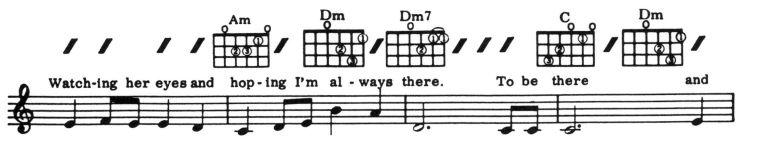

Watch-ing her eyes and hop-ing I'm al - ways there. To be there and

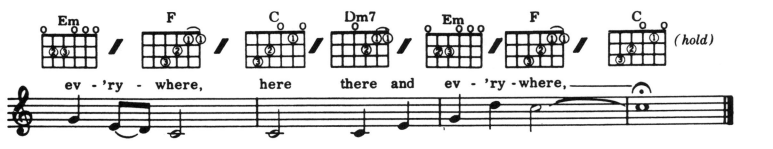

ev - 'ry - where, here there and ev -'ry-where, _____ (hold)

HEY JUDE

By JOHN LENNON and PAUL McCARTNEY

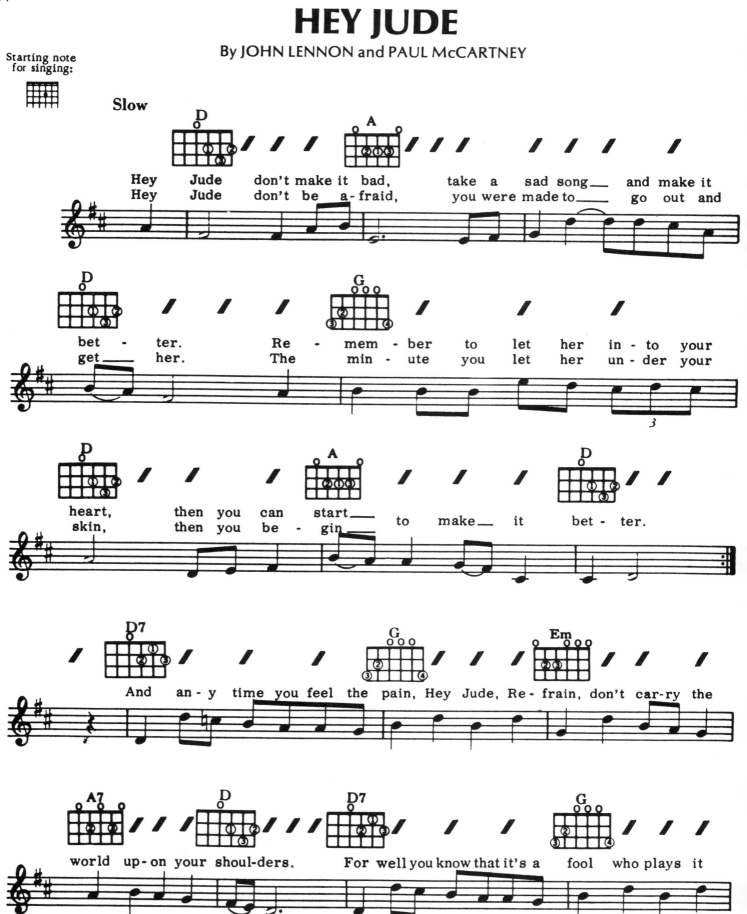

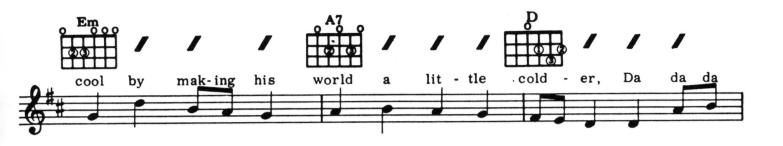

cool by mak-ing his world a lit-tle cold-er, Da da da

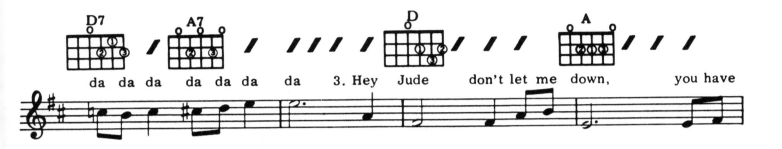

da da da da da da da 3. Hey Jude don't let me down, you have

found her, now go and get her. Re-mem-ber to let her in-to your

heart, then you can start to make it bet-ter.

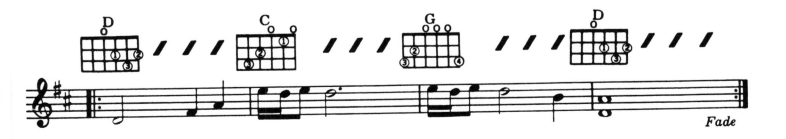

Fade

I AM THE WALRUS

By JOHN LENNON and PAUL McCARTNEY

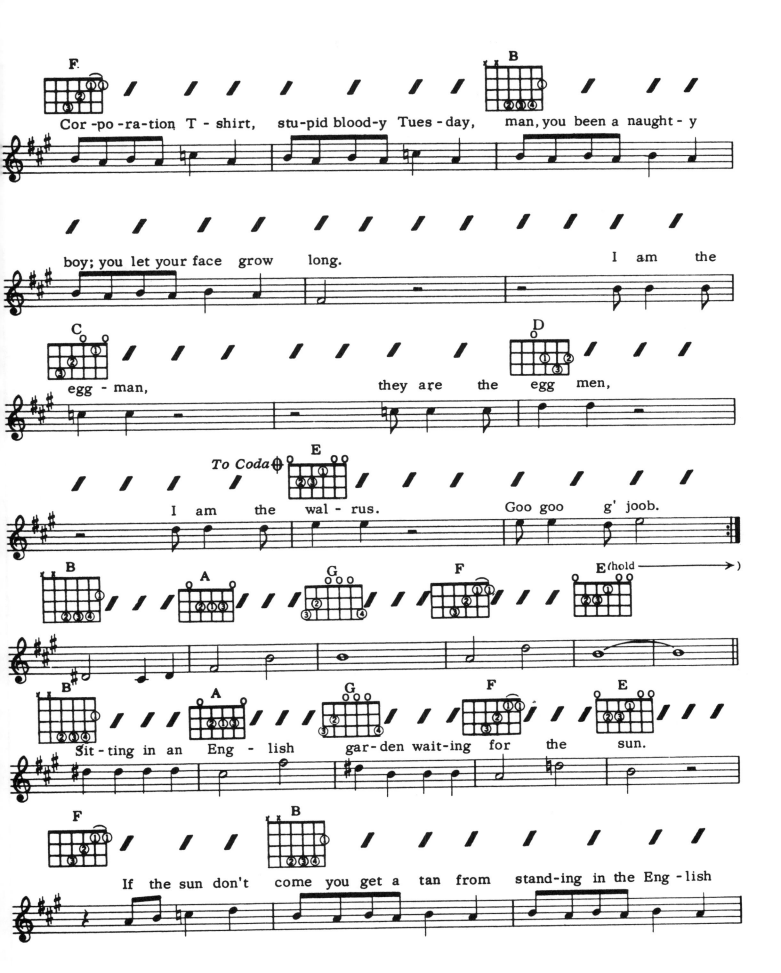

2. Mr. City Policeman sitting pretty, little policemen in a row.
   See how they fly like Lucy in the sky, see how they run.
   I'm crying.
   Yellow matter custard dripping from a dead dog's eye.
   Crab-a-locker fish-wife pornographic priestess,
   Boy, you been a naughty girl; you let your knickers down.
   I am the eggman, (etc.)
   Sitting in an English garden (etc.)

3. Expert texpert choking smokers; don't you think the joker laughs at you?
   See how they smile like pigs in a sty, see how they snied.
   I'm crying.
   Semolina pilchards climbing up the Eiffel Tower.
   Elementary penguins singing Hare Krishna,
   Man, you should have seen them kicking Edgar Allan Poe.
   I am the eggman, (etc.)

I DON'T WANT TO SPOIL THE PARTY

By JOHN LENNON and PAUL McCARTNEY

I CALL YOUR NAME

By JOHN LENNON and PAUL McCARTNEY

I FEEL FINE

By JOHN LENNON and PAUL McCARTNEY

I NEED YOU

By GEORGE HARRISON

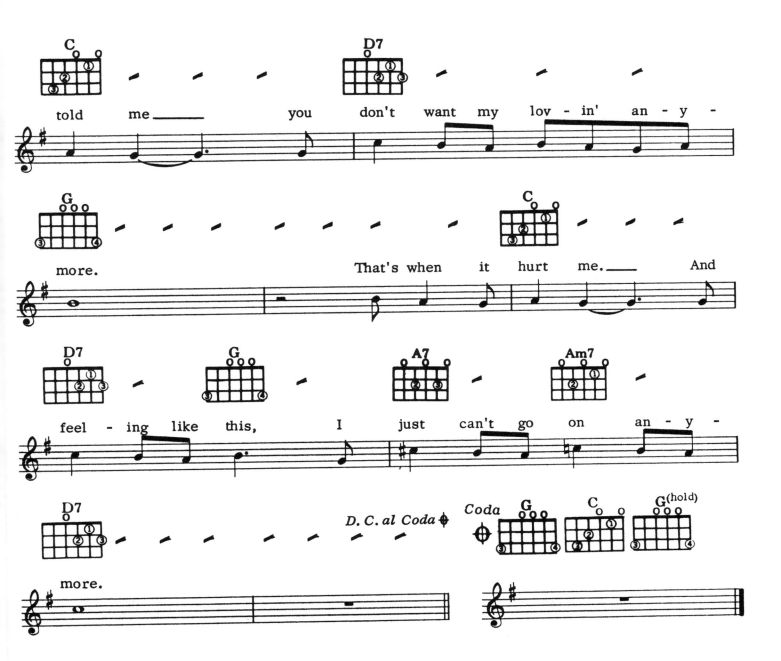

2. Said you had a thing or two to tell me.
   How was I to know you would upset me.
   I didn't realize; as I looked in your eyes
   You told me.
   Oh yes, you told me *(etc.)*

3. Please remember how I feel about you.
   I could never really live without you.
   So come on back and see just what you mean to me.
   I need you.

I SHOULD HAVE KNOWN BETTER

By JOHN LENNON and PAUL McCARTNEY

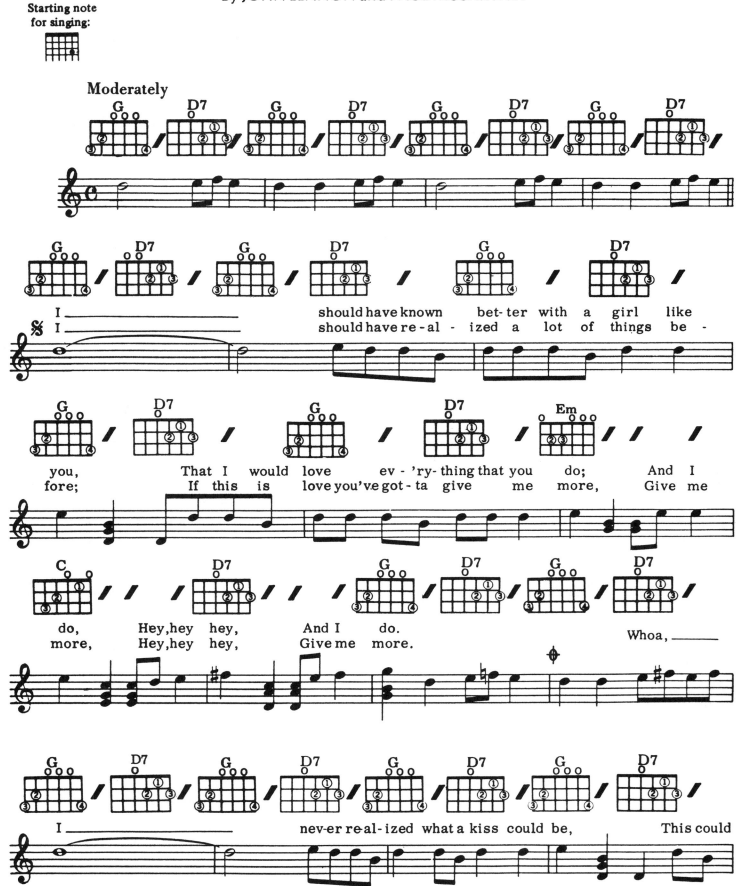

I WANT TO TELL YOU

By GEORGE HARRISON

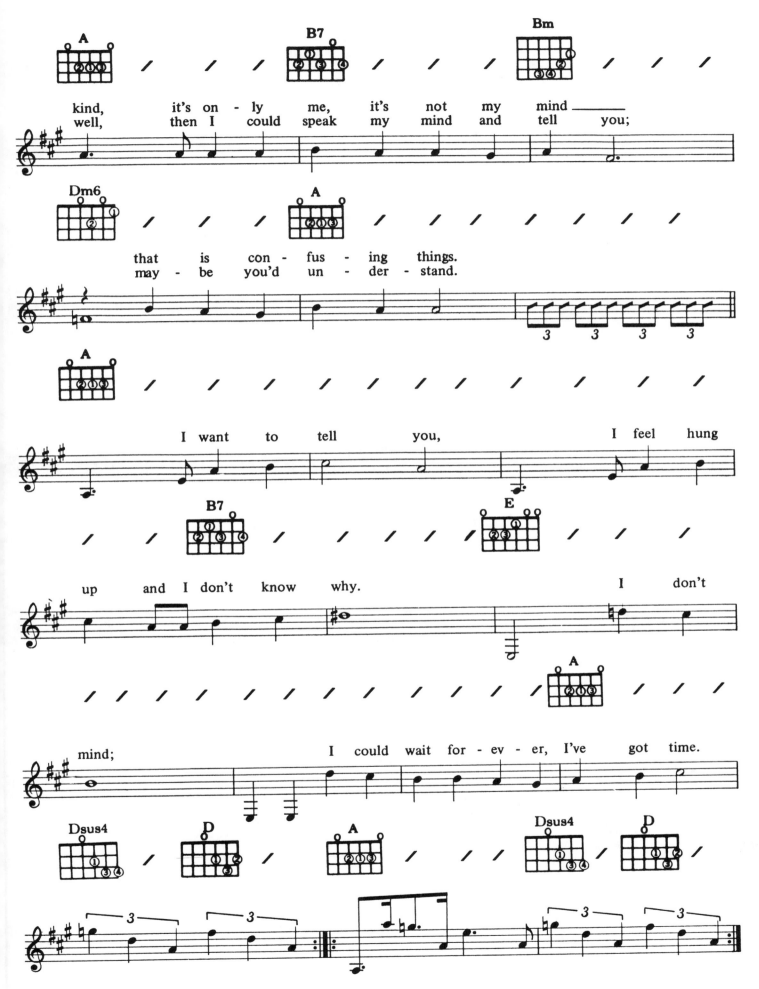

I WANT YOU
(She's So Heavy)

By JOHN LENNON and PAUL McCARTNEY

Starting note
for singing:

I WILL

By JOHN LENNON and PAUL McCARTNEY

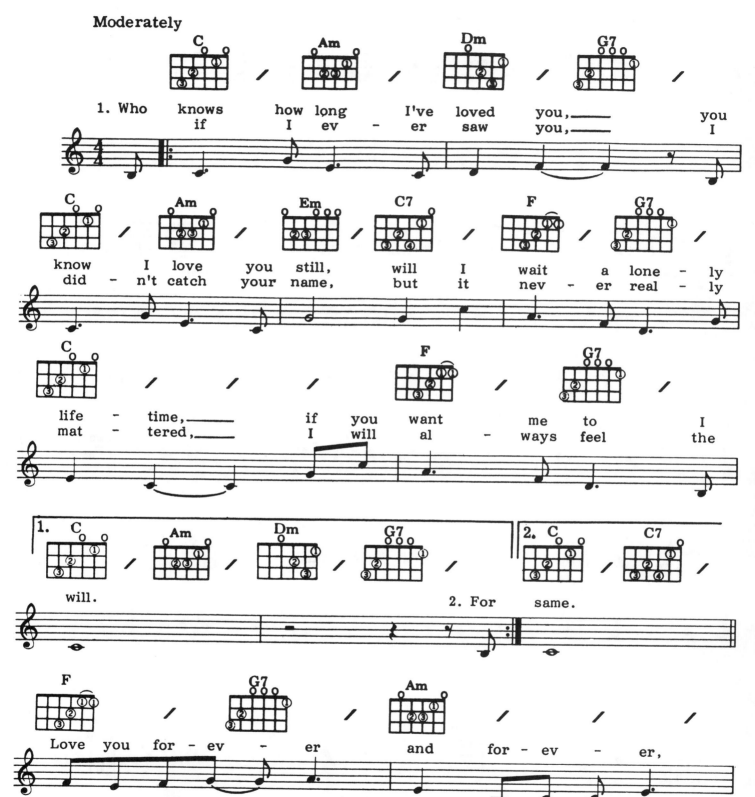

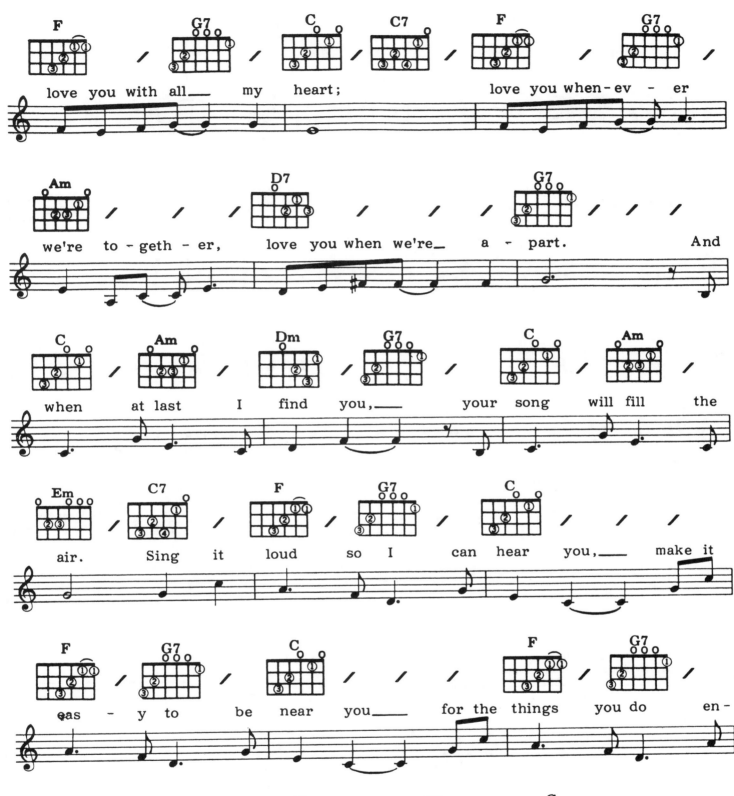

love you with all__ my heart; love you when-ev - er we're to-geth - er, love you when we're__ a - part. And when at last I find you,__ your song will fill the air. Sing it loud so I can hear you,__ make it

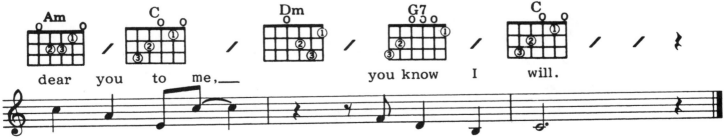

eas - y to be near you__ for the things you do en- dear you to me,__ you know I will.

I'LL BE BACK

By JOHN LENNON and PAUL McCARTNEY

Moderately

I'LL CRY INSTEAD

By JOHN LENNON and PAUL McCARTNEY

Starting note for singing

Moderately

I've got ev-'ry rea-son on earth to be mad,
chip on my shoul-der that's big-ger than my feet,

'Cause I've just lost the on-ly girl I had.
I can't talk to peo-ple that I meet.

If I could get my way, I'd get my-self locked
If I could see you now, I'd try to make you

up to-day, But I can't, so I cry in-stead.
say it some-how, But I can't, so I cry in-stead.

1.
I've got a

2.
No chord
Don't want to cry when there's peo-ple

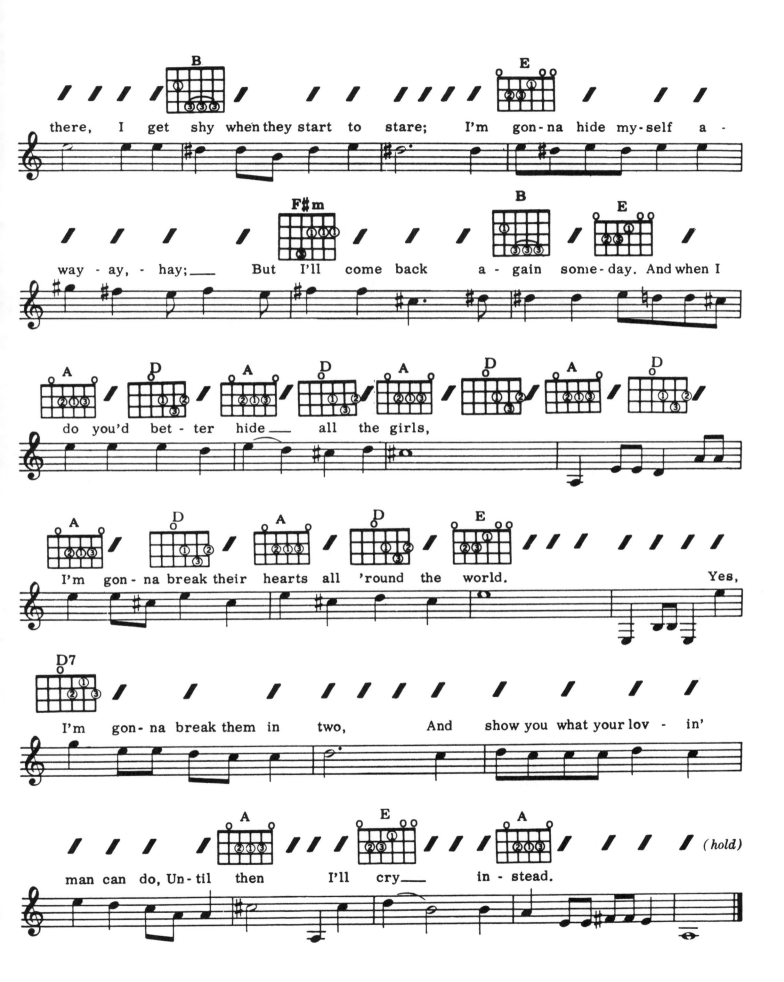

I'LL FOLLOW THE SUN

By JOHN LENNON and PAUL McCARTNEY

And now the time has come, and so, my love, I must go.

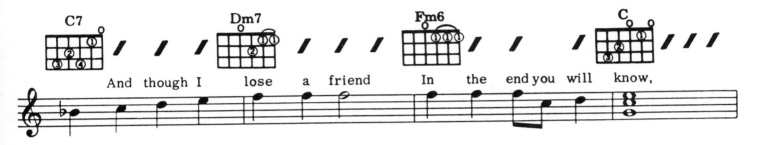

And though I lose a friend In the end you will know,

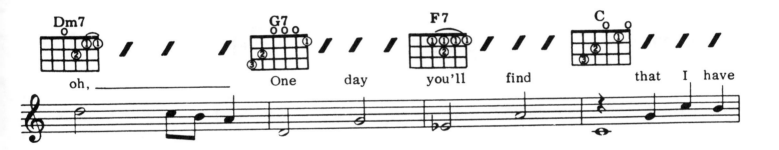

oh, _____ One day you'll find that I have

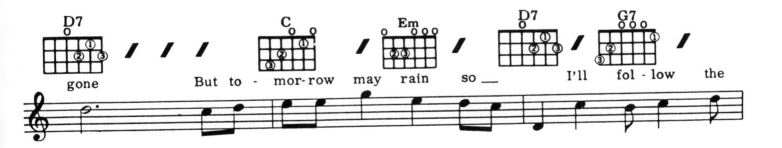

gone But to - mor - row may rain so __ I'll fol - low the

sun.

I'LL GET YOU

By JOHN LENNON and PAUL McCARTNEY

141

I'M A LOSER

By JOHN LENNON and PAUL McCARTNEY

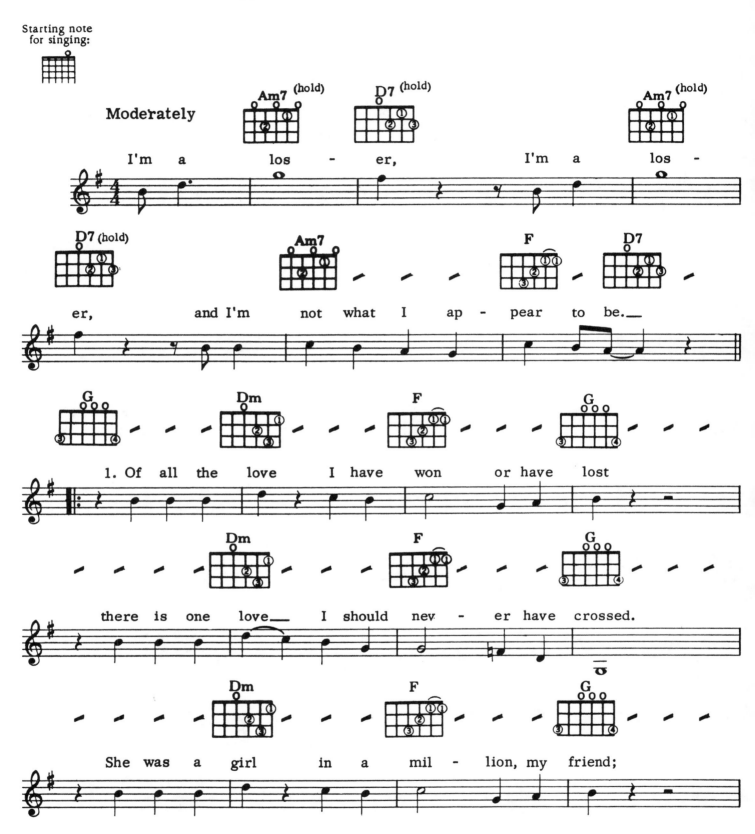

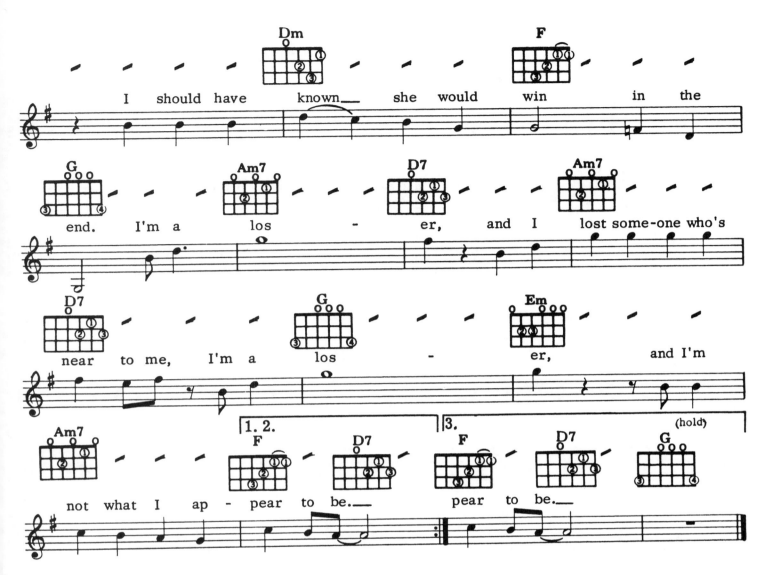

Dm · · · · · · · F · · ·
I should have known___ she would win in the

G · · Am7 · · D7 · · Am7 · ·
end. I'm a los - er, and I lost some-one who's

D7 · · · G · · Em · ·
near to me, I'm a los - er, and I'm

Am7 · · 1. 2. F D7 3. F D7 (hold) G
not what I ap - pear to be.___ pear to be.___

2. Although I laugh
   And I act like a clown
   Beneath this mask
   I am wearing a frown.

   My tears are falling
   Like rain from the sky
   Is it for her
   Or myself that I cry.

   I'm a loser
   And I lost someone who's near to me
   I'm a loser
   And I'm not what I appear to be.

3. What have I done
   To deserve such a fate
   I realize
   I have left it too late.

   And so it's true
   Pride comes before a fall
   I'm telling you
   So that you won't lose all

   I'm a loser *(etc.)*

I'M DOWN

By JOHN LENNON and PAUL McCARTNEY

Starting note for singing:

Fast

1. You tell lies think-ing I can't see___ You can't cry 'cause you're
2. Man buys ring, wom-an throws it a-way Same old thing hap-pen

laugh-in' at me___ I'm down___ I'm down___
ev-er-y day___ }

I'm down.___

How can you laugh___ when you

know I'm down___ (how can you laugh___) when you know I'm down.___

3. know I'm down.___ I said I'm down.___ I'm real-ly

down. I'm real-ly down. I'm real-ly down.___

3. We're all alone and there's nobody else.
   She'll still moan: "Keep your hands to yourself."
   I'm down (etc.)

I'M LOOKING THROUGH YOU
By JOHN LENNON and PAUL McCARTNEY

3. Your thinking of me in the same old way.
You were above me, but not today.
The only difference is you're down there;
I'm looking through you, and you're nowhere.

I'M HAPPY JUST TO DANCE WITH YOU

By JOHN LENNON and PAUL McCARTNEY

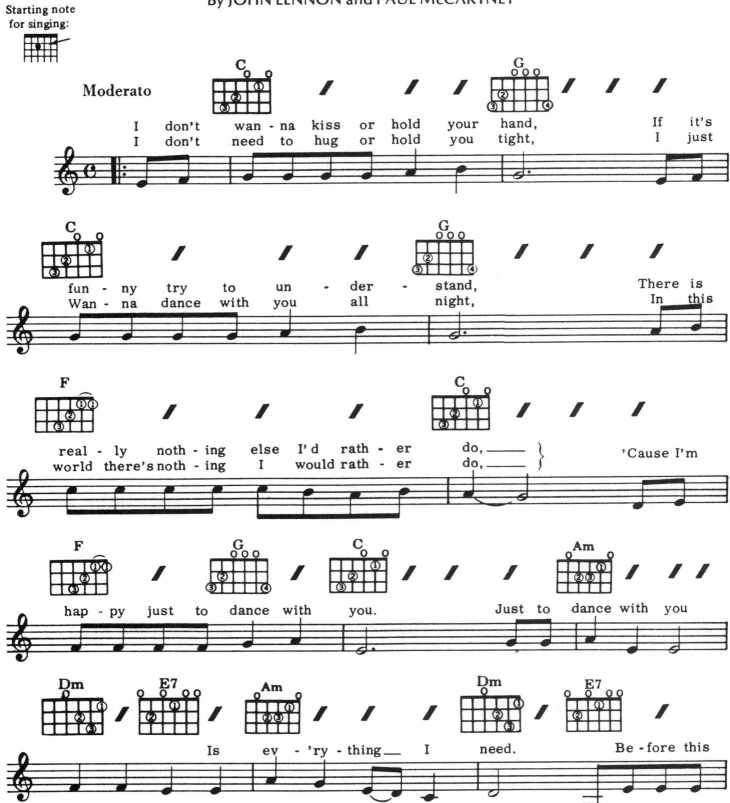

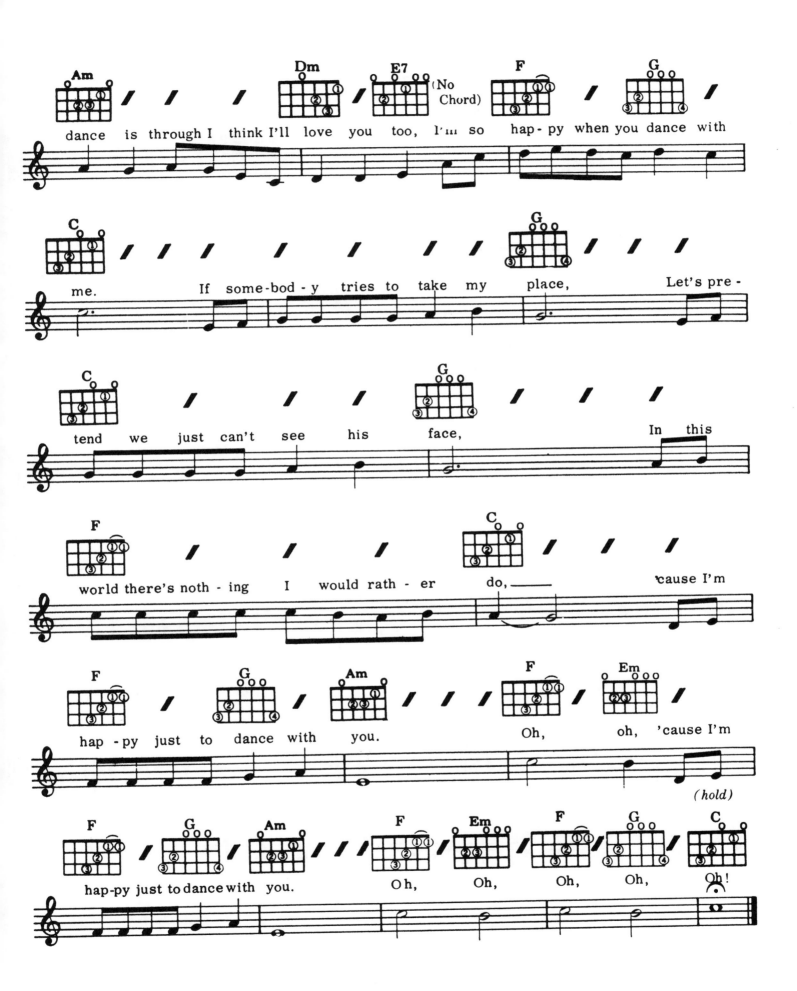

I'M ONLY SLEEPING

By JOHN LENNON and PAUL McCARTNEY

Starting note
for singing:

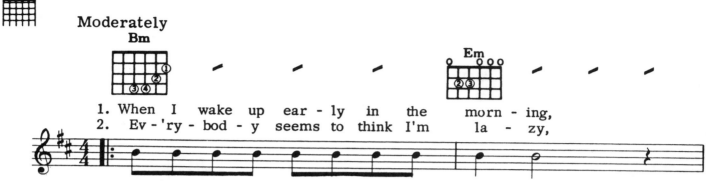

Moderately

1. When I wake up ear - ly in the morn - ing,
2. Ev - 'ry - bod - y seems to think I'm la - zy,

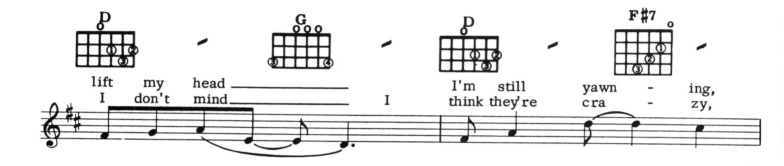

lift my head _____
I don't mind _____   I   I'm still   yawn - ing,
think they're   cra - zy,

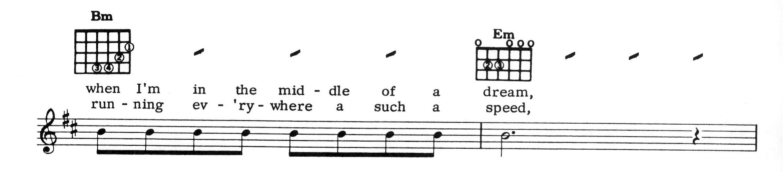

when I'm   in the mid - dle   of a   dream,
run - ning   ev - 'ry - where a   such a   speed,

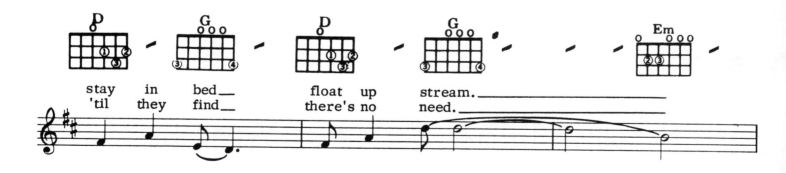

stay   in   bed__   float up   stream. _____
'til   they   find__   there's no   need. _____

Please don't wake me no, don't shake me, leave me where I
Please don't spoil my day, I'm miles a - way and af - ter

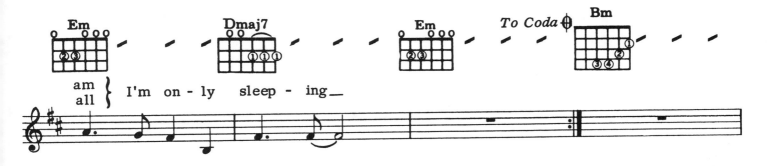

am
all } I'm on - ly sleep - ing

To Coda

Keep-ing an eye on the world go-ing by my

win - dow, tak - ing my time.

D.C. al Coda   Coda

3. Lying there and staring at the ceiling, waiting for a sleepy feeling.
   (Guitar Solo) _____
   Please don't spoil my day, I'm miles away and after all
   I'm only sleeping.

I'M SO TIRED

By JOHN LENNON and PAUL McCARTNEY

Starting note for singing:

IF I FELL

By JOHN LENNON and PAUL McCARTNEY

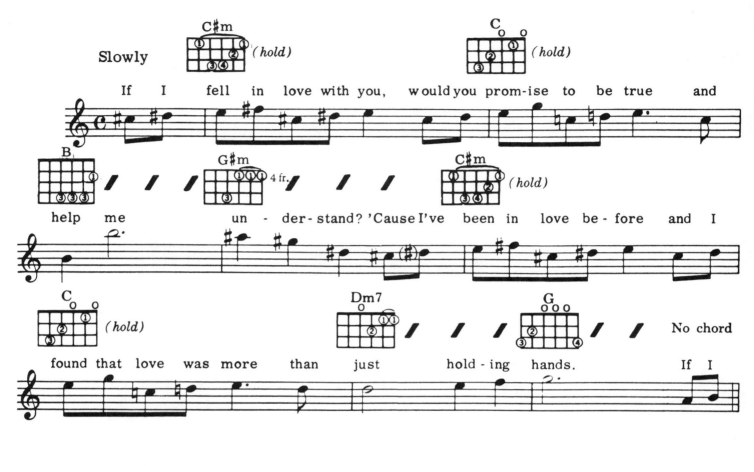

Slowly

C#m (hold)   C (hold)

If I fell in love with you, would you prom-ise to be true and

B   G#m 4 fr.   C#m (hold)

help me un-der-stand? 'Cause I've been in love be-fore and I

C (hold)   Dm7   G   No chord

found that love was more than just hold-ing hands. If I

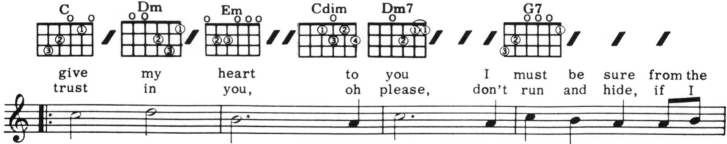

C   Dm   Em   Cdim   Dm7   G7

give my heart to you, I must be sure from the
trust in you, oh please, don't run and hide, if I

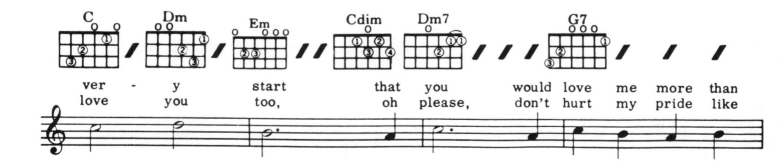

C   Dm   Em   Cdim   Dm7   G7

ver - y start that you would love me more than
love you too, oh please, don't hurt my pride like

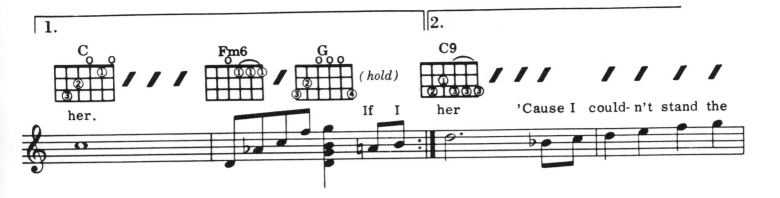

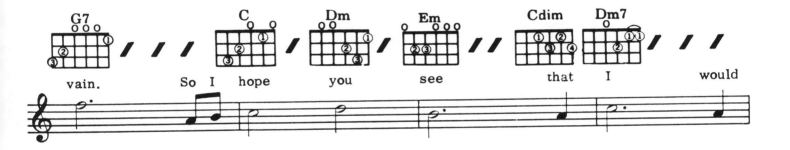

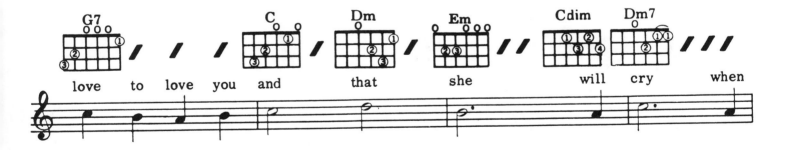

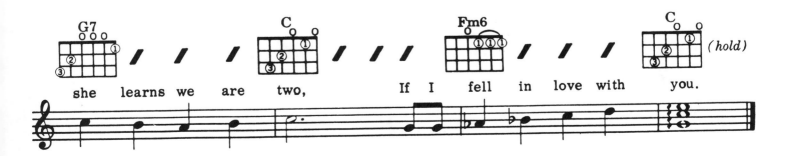

1. C ... Fm6 ... G (hold)

her. ... If I

2. C9

her 'Cause I could-n't stand the

F ... Fm6 ... C

pain, and I would be sad if our new love was in

G7 ... C ... Dm ... Em ... Cdim ... Dm7

vain. So I hope you see that I would

G7 ... C ... Dm ... Em ... Cdim ... Dm7

love to love you and that she will cry when

G7 ... C ... Fm6 ... C (hold)

she learns we are two, If I fell in love with you.

IF I NEEDED SOMEONE

By GEORGE HARRISON

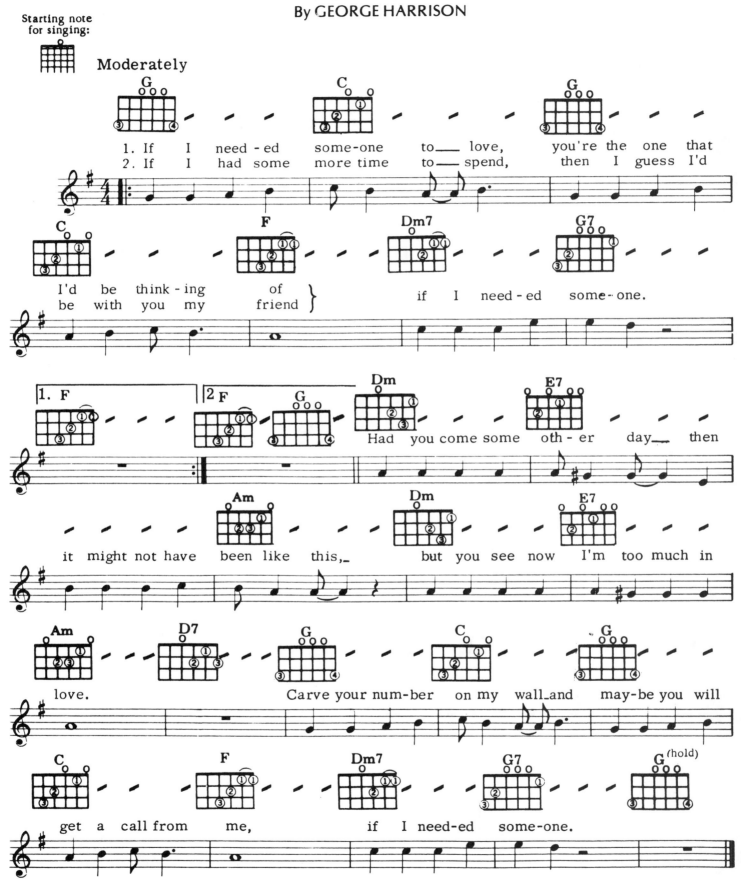

THE INNER LIGHT

By GEORGE HARRISON

Starting note
for singing:

Slowly

G

1. With-out go-ing out of my door   I can
2. With-out go-ing out of your door   you can

G   G7   C   G   G7

know all things on earth.____   With - out look-ing out of my
know all things on earth.____   With - out look-ing out of your

C   G   G7   C

win - dow   you can know the ways of   heav - en; } The
win - dow   you can know the ways of   heav - en;

G   F

far-ther one trav - els,____   the less one knows,____   the

G   C   G   (No chords)

less one knows.____   Ar-

rive with-out trav-el -ing,____   See all with-out look - ing.____

IN MY LIFE

By JOHN LENNON and PAUL McCARTNEY

Starting note for singing:

IT WON'T BE LONG

By PAUL McCARTNEY

159

long yeah, yeah, yeah, it won't be long_ yeah, yeah,

yeah, it won't be long yeah, 'till I be-long to

you. Since you left me,

I'm so a-lone_ now you're com-ing,_ you're com-ing on home,_

I'll be good like I know_ I should_ you're com-ing home, you're com-ing

1. home._
2. home._

I be-long to_ you.

3. Ev'ry day we'll be happy I know,
   Now I know that you won't leave me no more.
   It won't be long, yeah. *(etc.)*

IT'S ALL TOO MUCH

By GEORGE HARRISON

2. Floating down the stream of time
From life to life with me.
Makes no difference where you are
Or where you'd like to be.
It's all too much for me to take
The love that's shining all around you.
All the world is birthday cake
So take a piece but not too much.

3. Sail me on a silver sun,
Where I know that I'm free.
Show me that I'm everywhere
And get me home for tea.
It's all too much for me to take
There's plenty there for everybody.
The more you give the more you get
The more it is and it's too much.

IT'S ONLY LOVE

By JOHN LENNON and PAUL McCARTNEY

Starting note for singing:

Slowly

I get high when I see you go by, my, oh my,
Is it right that you and I should fight ev-'ry night?

When you sigh my my in-side just flies, But-ter-flies
Just the sight of you makes night-time bright, Ver-y bright

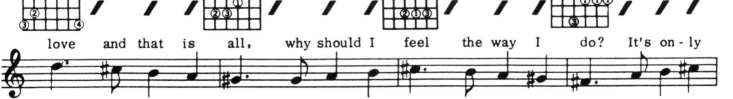

Why am I so shy when I'm be-side you}
Have-n't I the right to make it up, girl?} It's on-ly

love and that is all, why should I feel the way I do? It's on-ly

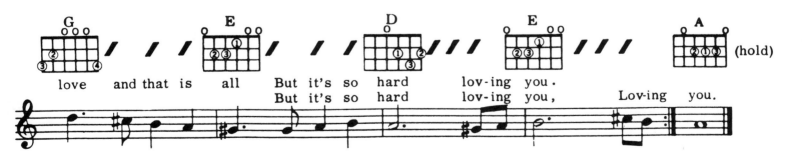

love and that is all But it's so hard lov-ing you.
But it's so hard lov-ing you, Lov-ing you.

I'VE GOT A FEELING

By JOHN LENNON and PAUL McCARTNEY

Moderately slow

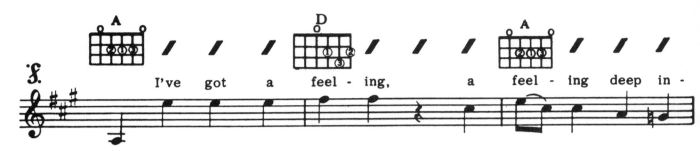

I've got a feel - ing, a feel - ing deep in -

side, oh yeah, oh

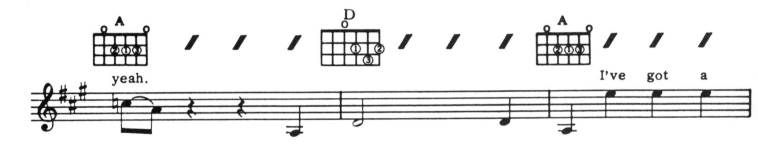

yeah. I've got a

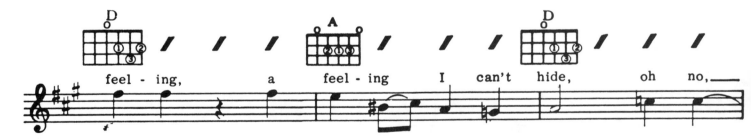

feel - ing, a feel - ing I can't hide, oh no, ____

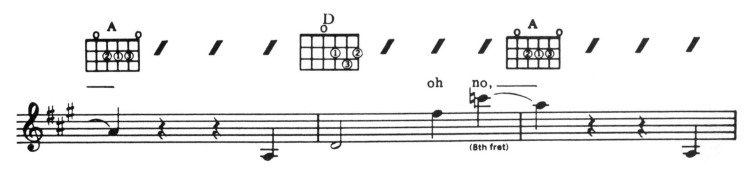

oh no, ____

(8th fret)

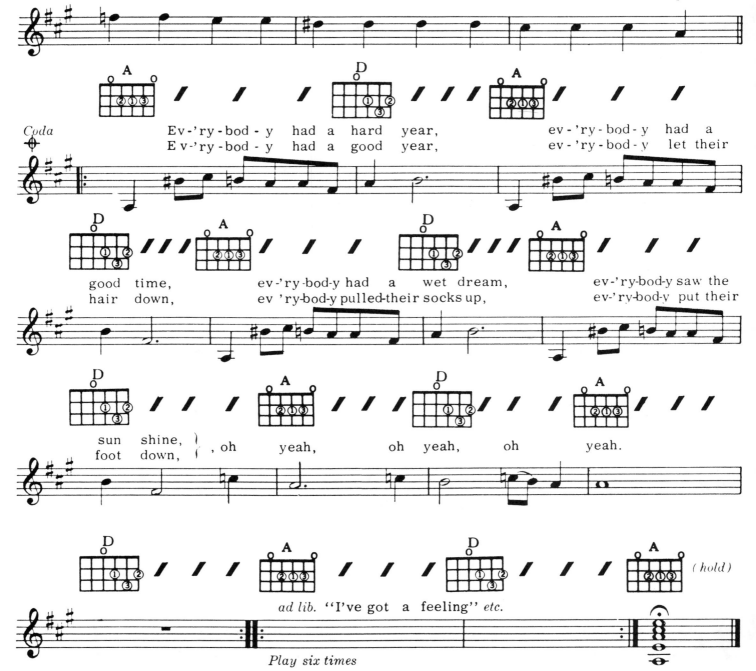

Coda

Ev-'ry-bod-y had a hard year, ev-'ry-bod-y had a
Ev-'ry-bod-y had a good year, ev-'ry-bod-y let their

good time, ev-'ry-bod-y had a wet dream, ev-'ry-bod-y saw the
hair down, ev-'ry-bod-y pulled their socks up, ev-'ry-bod-y put their

sun shine, } , oh yeah, oh yeah, oh yeah.
foot down, }

ad lib. "I've got a feeling" *etc.*

(hold)

Play six times

Oh please believe me I'd hate to miss the train, oh yeah, oh yeah,
And if you leave me I won't be late again, oh no, oh no, oh no.
Yeah, Yeah, I've got a feeling, yeah!

I've got a feeling that keeps me on my toes, oh yeah, oh yeah.
I've got a feeling, I think that everybody knows, oh yeah, oh yeah, oh yeah.
Yeah, Yeah, I've got a feeling yeah!

I'VE JUST SEEN A FACE

By JOHN LENNON and PAUL McCARTNEY

JULIA

By JOHN LENNON and PAUL McCARTNEY

Starting note
for singing:

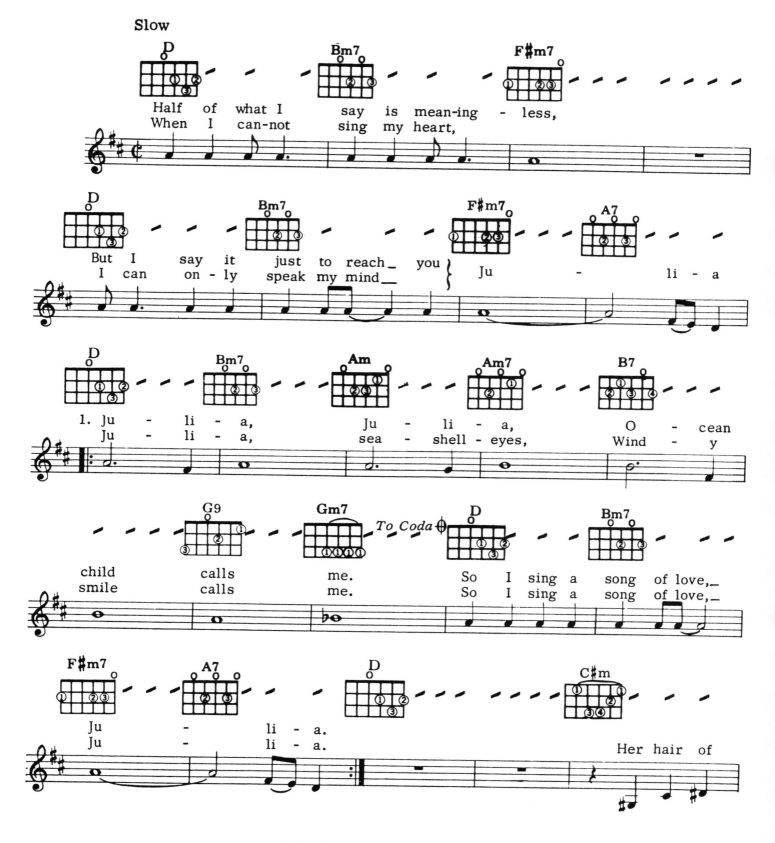

2. Julia; Sleeping sand,
Silent cloud touch me.
So I sing a song of love for Julia, Julia, Julia.

LADY MADONNA

By JOHN LENNON and PAUL McCARTNEY

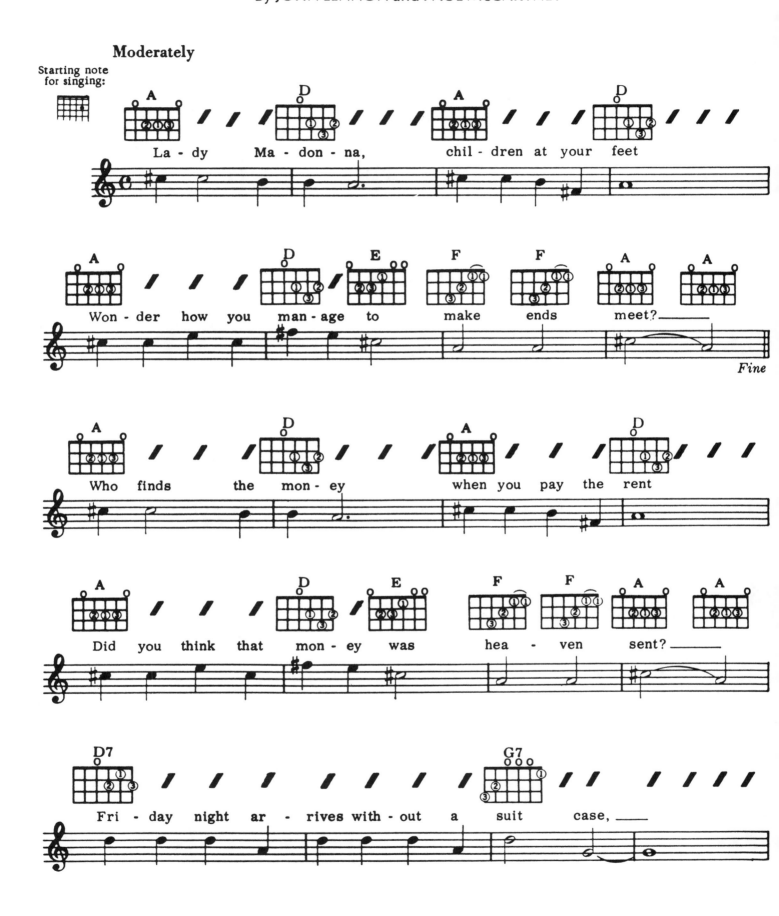

C

Am

Sun - day morn - ing creep - ing like a nun.

D7

G7

Mon - day's child has learned to tie his shoe - lace. ____

C

Bm

Bm

E7

See how they run. ____

D.C. al Fine

Lady Madonna, baby at your breast,
Wonder how you manage to feed the rest.
Lady Madonna lying on the bed,
Listen to the music playing in your head.

Tuesday afternoon is never ending,
Wednesday morning papers didn't come,
Thursday night your stocking needed mending,
See how they run.

LET IT BE

By JOHN LENNON and PAUL McCARTNEY

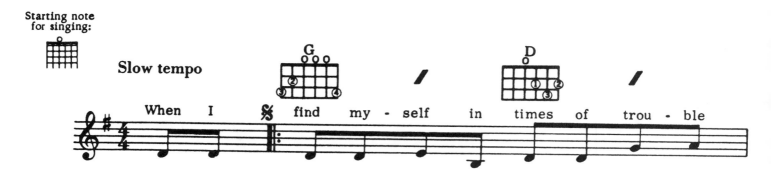

Starting note for singing:

Slow tempo

When I §| find my - self in times of trou - ble

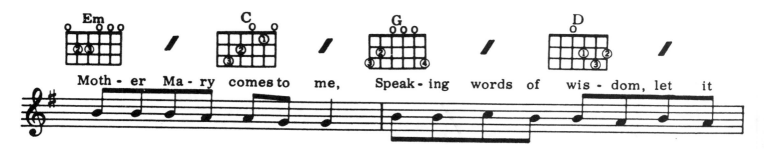

Moth - er Ma - ry comes to me, Speak - ing words of wis - dom, let it

be. ____ And in my hour of dark-ness she is

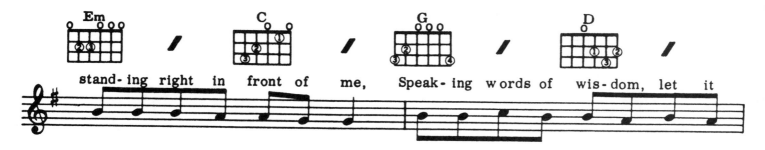

stand - ing right in front of me, Speak - ing words of wis - dom, let it

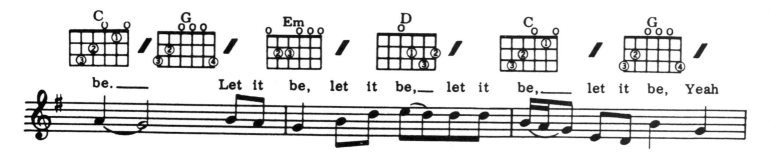

be. ____ Let it be, let it be,__ let it be,__ let it be, Yeah

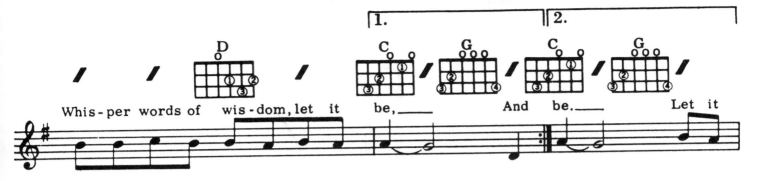

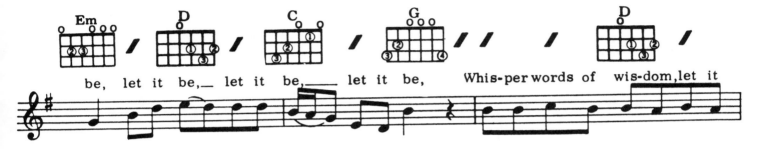

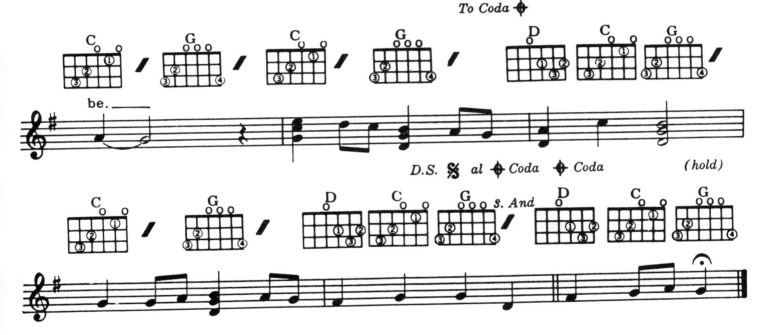

2. And when the broken hearted people
   Living in the world agree,
   There will be an answer, let it be.
   For tho' they may be parted
   There is still a chance that they will see,
   There will be an answer, let it be.
   Let it be, let it be, let it be, let it be,
   Yeah There will be an answer, let it be.
   Let it be, let it be, let it, be, let it be,
   Whisper words of wisdom, let it be.

3. And when the night is cloudy
   There is still a light that shines on me,
   Shine until tomorrow, let it be.
   I wake up to the sound of music
   Mother Mary comes to me,
   Speaking words of wisdom, let it be.
   Let it be, let it be, let it be, let it be,
   Yeah There will be an answer, let it be.
   Let it be, let it be, let it be, let it be,
   Whisper words of wisdom, let it be.

LITTLE CHILD

By JOHN LENNON and PAUL McCARTNEY

Starting note
for singing:

Moderately

Lit - tle child, lit - tle child, lit - tle

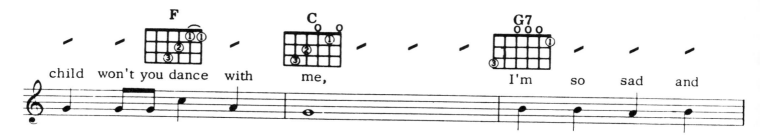

child won't you dance with me, I'm so sad and

lone - ly, ba - by take a chance with me. Lit - tle

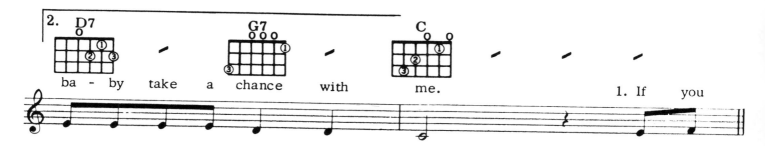

ba - by take a chance with me. 1. If you

want some - one to make you feel so fine, ___ then we'll
by my side ___ you're the on - ly one, ___ don't you

The Long and Winding Road

By JOHN LENNON and PAUL McCARTNEY

Starting note for singing:

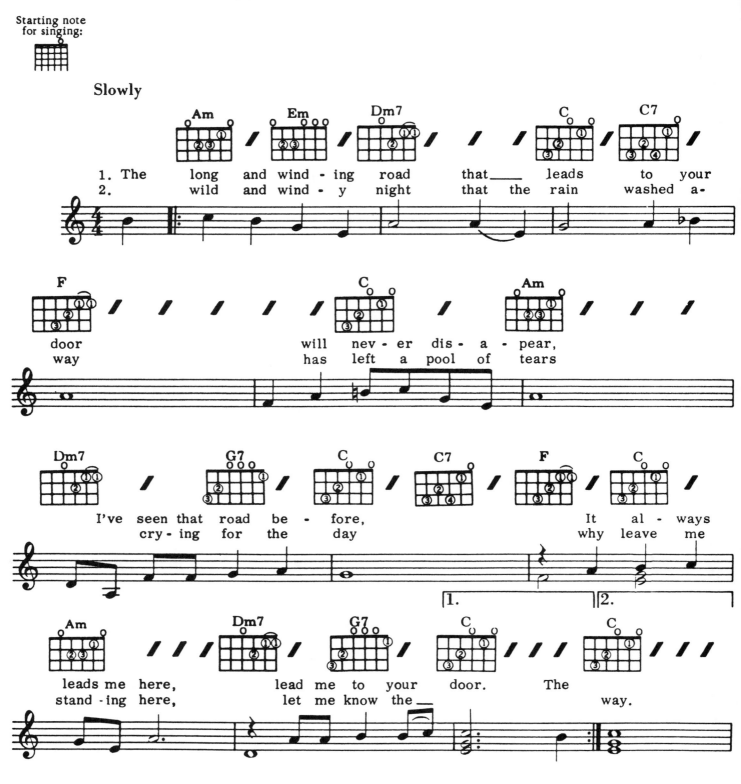

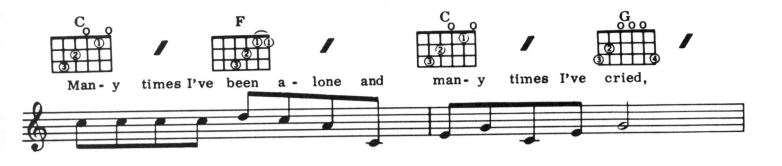

Man-y times I've been a-lone and man-y times I've cried,

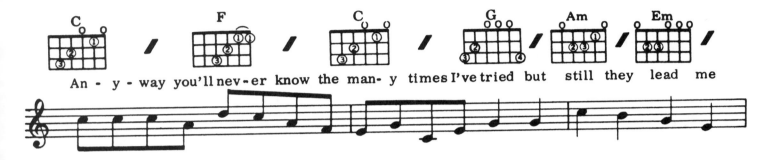

An-y-way you'll nev-er know the man-y times I've tried but still they lead me

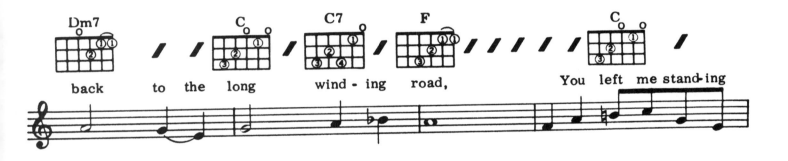

back to the long wind-ing road, You left me stand-ing

here, A long long time a-go Don't leave me

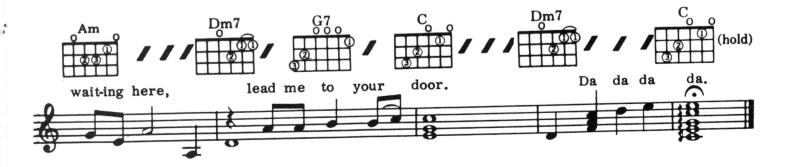

wait-ing here, lead me to your door. Da da da da. (hold)

LOVE YOU TO

By GEORGE HARRISON

Starting note
for singing:

Moderately

(No chords)

1. Each day just goes so fast, I turn a - round it's past, you don't get time to hang a sign on me.

Love me while you can,

Whole world in a plan.....

1. 2.   3.

2. A lifetime is so short,
   A new one can't be bought,
   Look what you've got
   Means such a lot to me.
   Make love all day long,
   Make love singing songs.

3. There's people standing 'round,
   Who'll screw you in the ground,
   They'll fill you in
   With all their sins you'll see.
   I'll make love to you,
   If you want me to.

LOVELY RITA

By JOHN LENNON and PAUL McCARTNEY

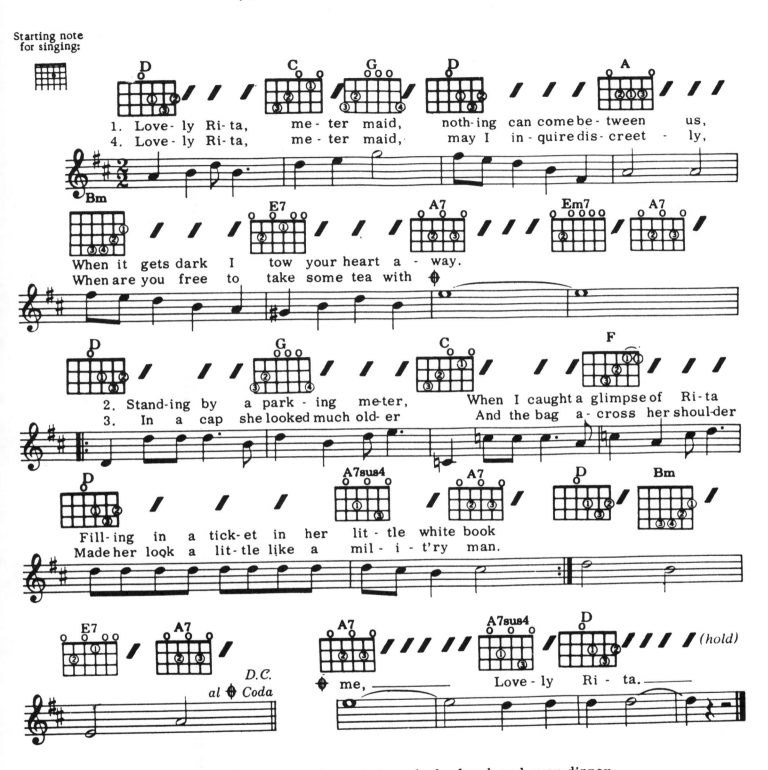

Took her out and tried to win her, had a laugh and over dinner
Told her I would really like to see her again.
Got the bill and Rita paid it, Took her home and nearly made it
Sitting on a sofa with a sister or two.
Lovely Rita, meter maid, where would I be without you?
Give us a wink and make me think of you, Lovely Rita.

LUCY IN THE SKY WITH DIAMONDS

By JOHN LENNON and PAUL McCARTNEY

Starting note for singing:

Moderately

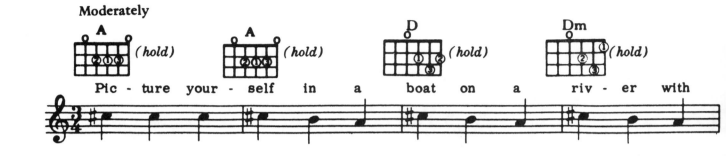

Pic - ture your - self in a boat on a riv - er with

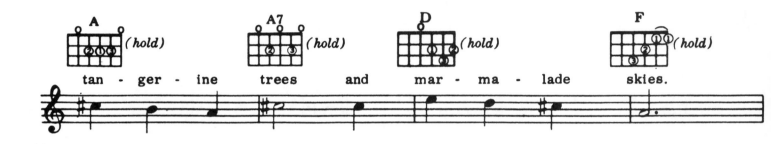

tan - ger - ine trees and mar - ma - lade skies.

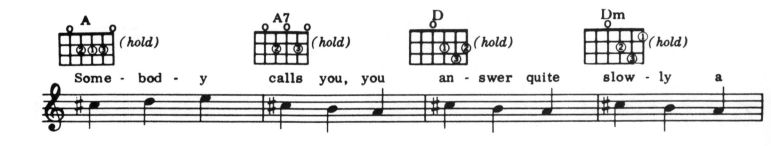

Some - bod - y calls you, you an - swer quite slow - ly a

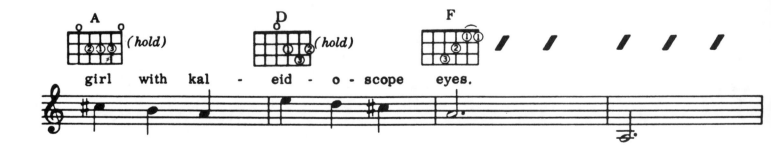

girl with kal - eid - o - scope eyes.

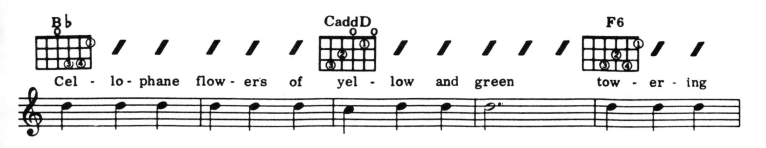

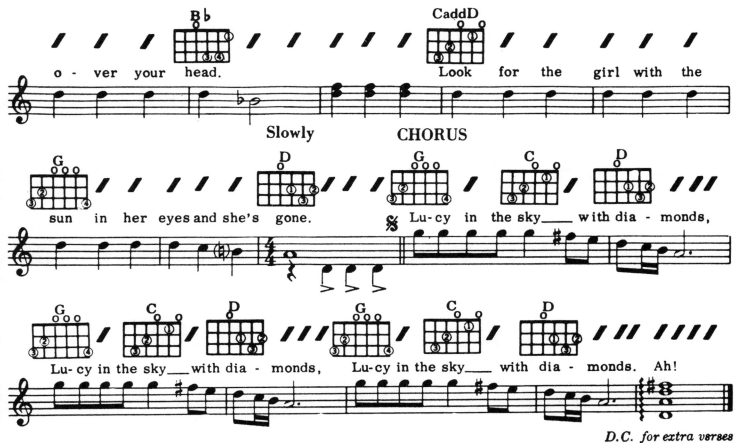

D.C. *for extra verses*
last time, D.S. and fade

Follow her down to a bridge by a fountain
Where rocking horse people eat marshmallow pies.
Ev'ryone smiles as you drift past the flowers
That grow so incredibly high.
Newspaper taxis appear on the shore waiting to take you away
Climb in the back with your head in the clouds and you're gone.

Chorus

Picture yourself on a train in a station
With plasticine porters with looking glass ties.
Suddenly someone is there at the turnstile
The girl with kaleidoscope eyes.

Chorus

MAGGIE MAE

Arrangement by JOHN LENNON, PAUL McCARTNEY, GEORGE HARRISON and RICHARD STARKEY

MEAN MR. MUSTARD

By JOHN LENNON and PAUL McCARTNEY

MAGICAL MYSTERY TOUR

By JOHN LENNON and PAUL McCARTNEY

Starting note
for singing:

MARTHA MY DEAR

By JOHN LENNON and PAUL McCARTNEY

MAXWELL'S SILVER HAMMER

By JOHN LENNON and PAUL McCARTNEY

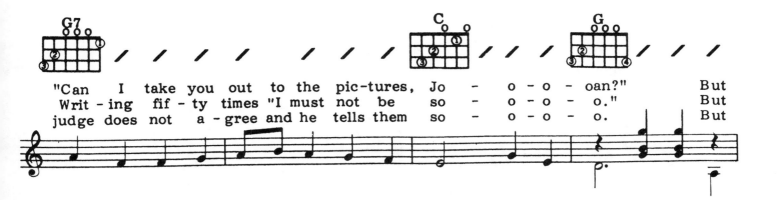

"Can I take you out to the pic-tures, Jo - o - o - oan?" But
Writ - ing fif - ty times "I must not be so - o - o - o." But
judge does not a - gree and he tells them so - o - o - o. But

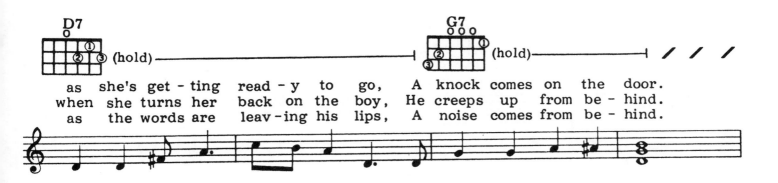

as she's get - ting read - y to go, A knock comes on the door.
when she turns her back on the boy, He creeps up from be - hind.
as the words are leav - ing his lips, A noise comes from be - hind.

Chorus

Bang! Bang! Max-well's sil - ver ham - mer came down up-on her head,
Bang! Bang! Max-well's sil - ver ham - mer came down up-on her head,
Bang! Bang! Max-well's sil - ver ham - mer came down up-on his head,

Clang! Clang! Max-well's sil - ver ham - mer made sure that she was dead.
Clang! Clang! Max-well's sil - ver ham - mer made sure that she was dead.
Clang! Clang! Max-well's sil - ver ham - mer made sure that he was dead.   *D.C.*

MICHELLE

By JOHN LENNON and PAUL McCARTNEY

Starting note for singing:

Moderately

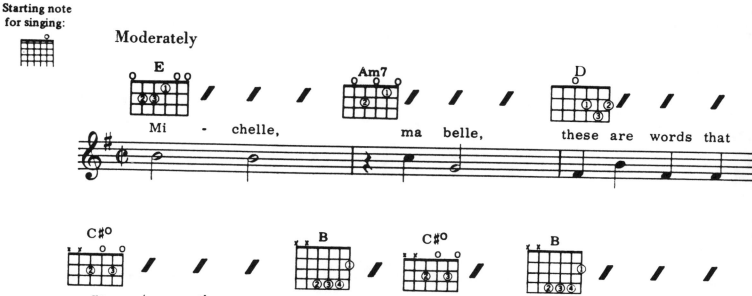

Mi - chelle, ma belle, these are words that

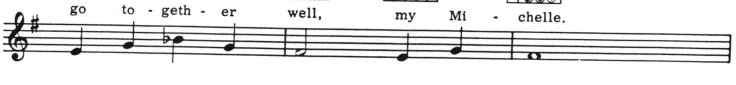

go to - geth - er well, my Mi - chelle.

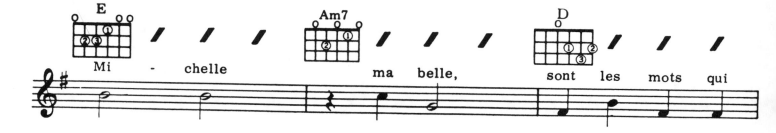

Mi - chelle ma belle, sont les mots qui

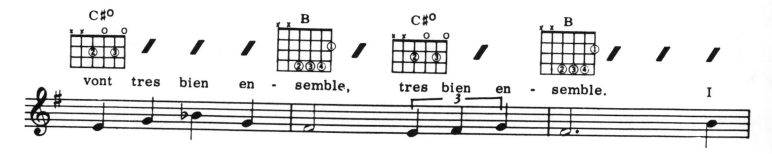

vont tres bien en - semble, tres bien en - semble.

189

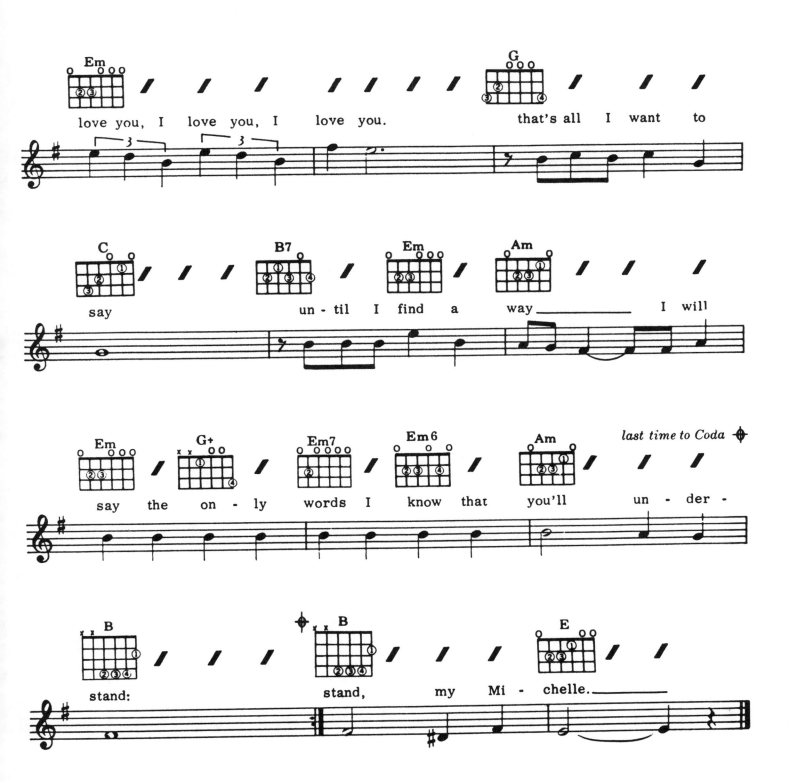

Michelle, ma belle, sont les mots qui vont tres bien ensemble, tres bien ensemble.
I need to, I need to, I need to, I need to make you see
Oh, what you mean to me. Until I do I'm hoping you will know what I mean.

I want you, I want you, I want you, I think you know by now
I'll get to you somehow. Until I do, I'm telling you so you'll understand,
My Michelle.

MOTHER NATURE'S SON

By JOHN LENNON and PAUL McCARTNEY

3. Find me in my field of grass,
   Mother nature's son.
   Swaying daisies, sing a lazy song beneath the sun.

THE NIGHT BEFORE

By JOHN LENNON and PAUL McCARTNEY

Starting note
for singing:

Moderately

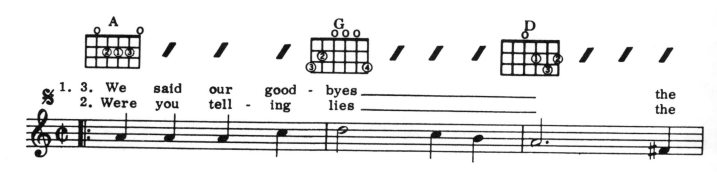

1. 3. We said our good - byes _____ the
2. Were you tell - ing lies _____ the

night be - fore, Love was in your eyes _____
night be - fore, Was I so un - wise _____

_____ the night be - fore. Now to - day I
_____ the night be - fore. When I held you

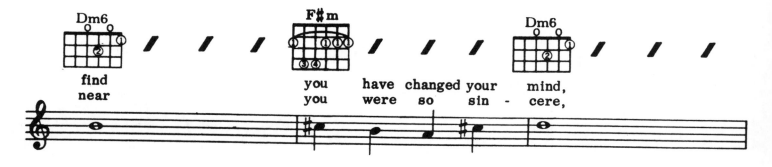

find you have changed your mind,
near you were so sin - cere,

Treat me like you did the night be - fore.

Last night is the night I will re -

mem - ber you by, When I think of

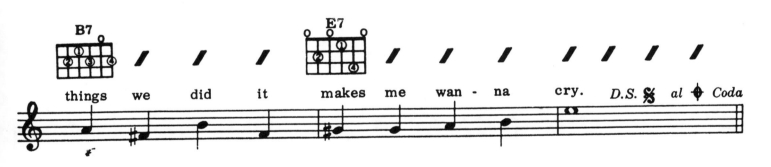

things we did it makes me wan - na cry. *D.S. ℅ al ◆ Coda*

◆ *Coda*

Like the night be - fore. *(hold)*

NO REPLY

By JOHN LENNON and PAUL McCARTNEY

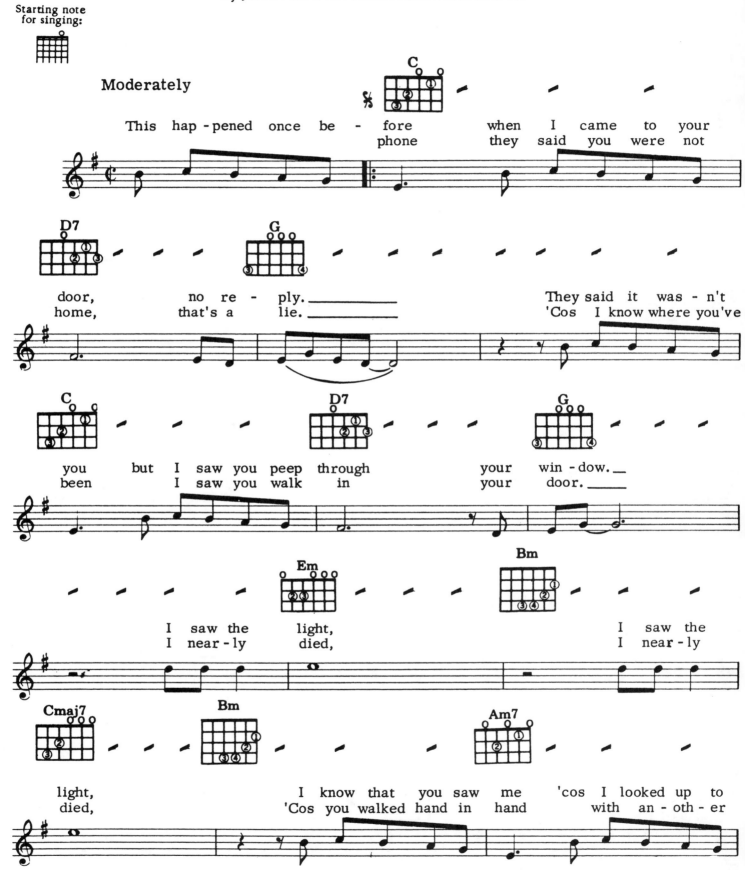

NORWEGIAN WOOD
(This Bird Has Flown)

By JOHN LENNON and PAUL McCARTNEY

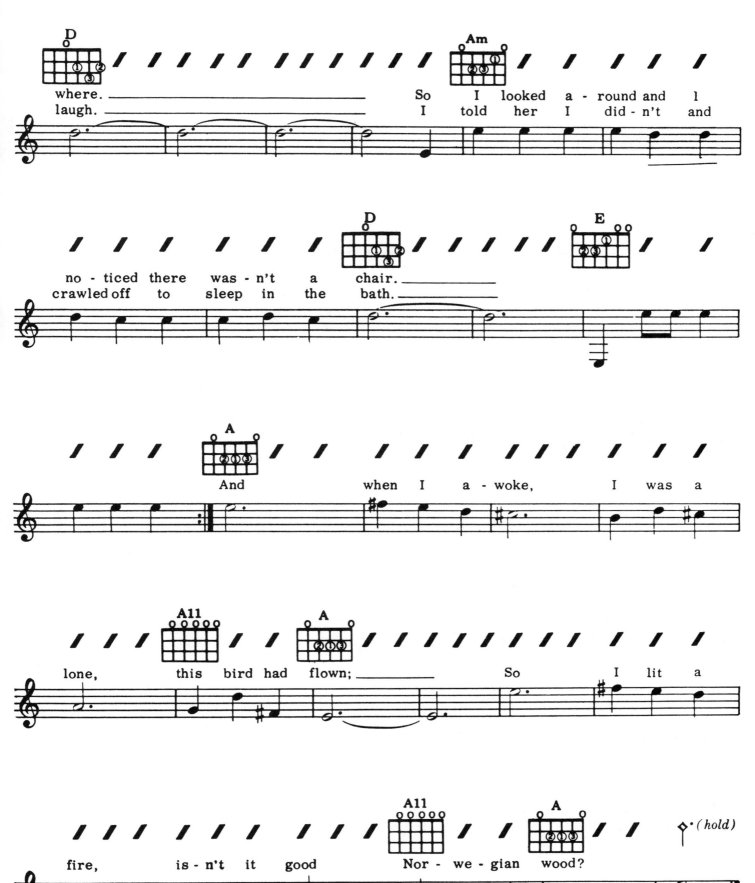

NOT A SECOND TIME

By JOHN LENNON and PAUL McCARTNEY

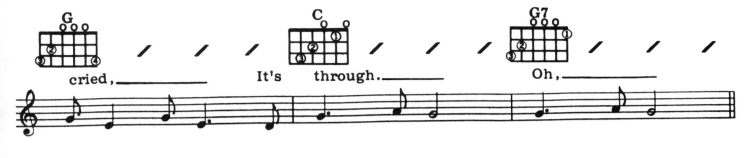

cried,_____ It's through._____ Oh,_____

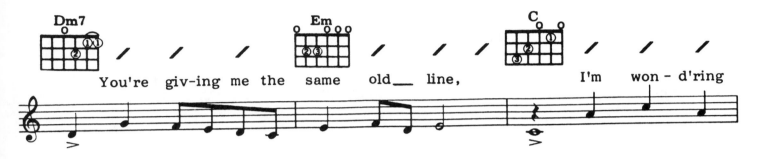

You're giv-ing me the same old__ line, I'm won-d'ring

why. You hurt me then, you're back a-gain,

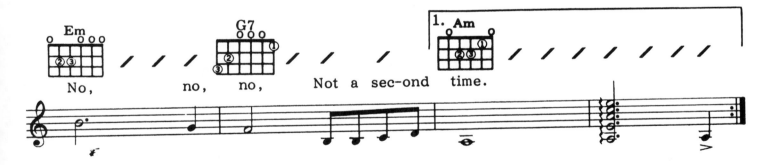

No, no, no, Not a sec-ond time.

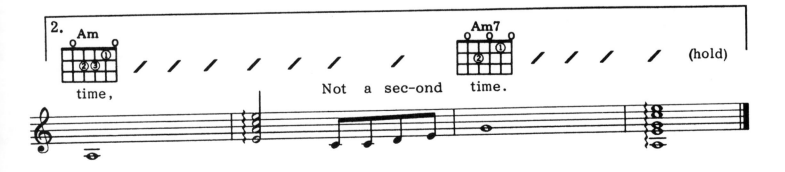

time, Not a sec-ond time. (hold)

NOWHERE MAN

By JOHN LENNON and PAUL McCARTNEY

Starting note
for singing:

Moderately Bright

1. 3. He's a real no - where man, Sit - ting in his
2. He's as blind as he can be, Just sees what he

No - where Land, Mak - ing all his no - where plans for
wants to see, No - where Man can you see me at

3rd time to Coda

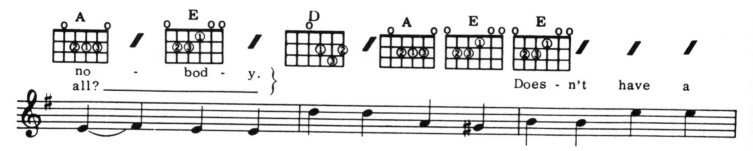

no - bod - y.
all? _____ } Does - n't have a

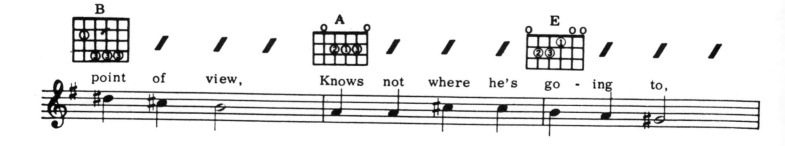

point of view, Knows not where he's go - ing to,

OB-LA-DI, OB-LA-DA

By JOHN LENNON and PAUL McCARTNEY

Starting note for singing:

Moderately Bright

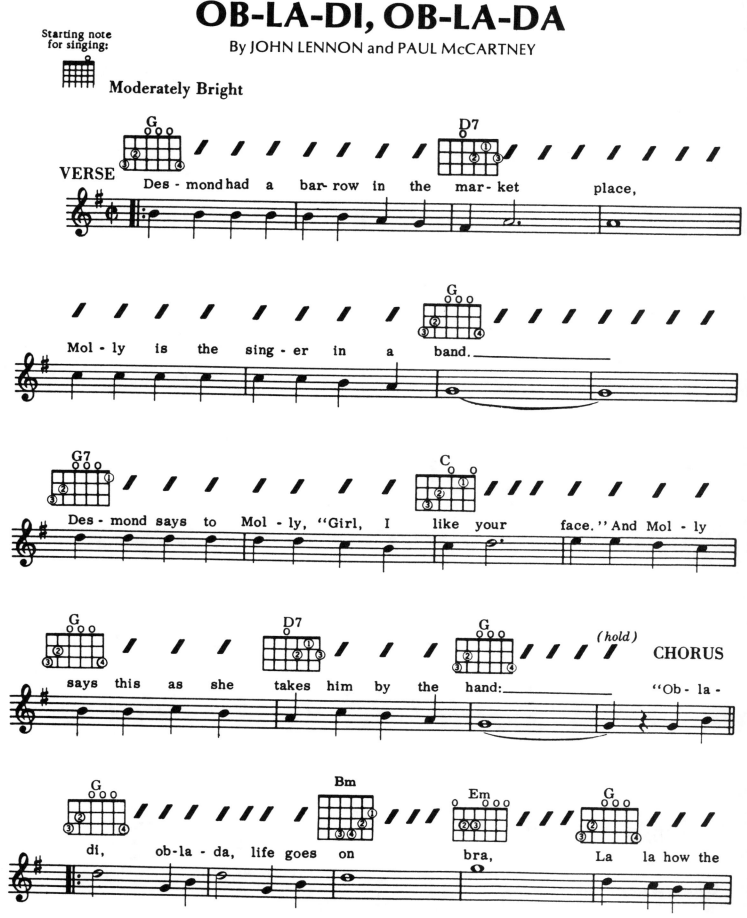

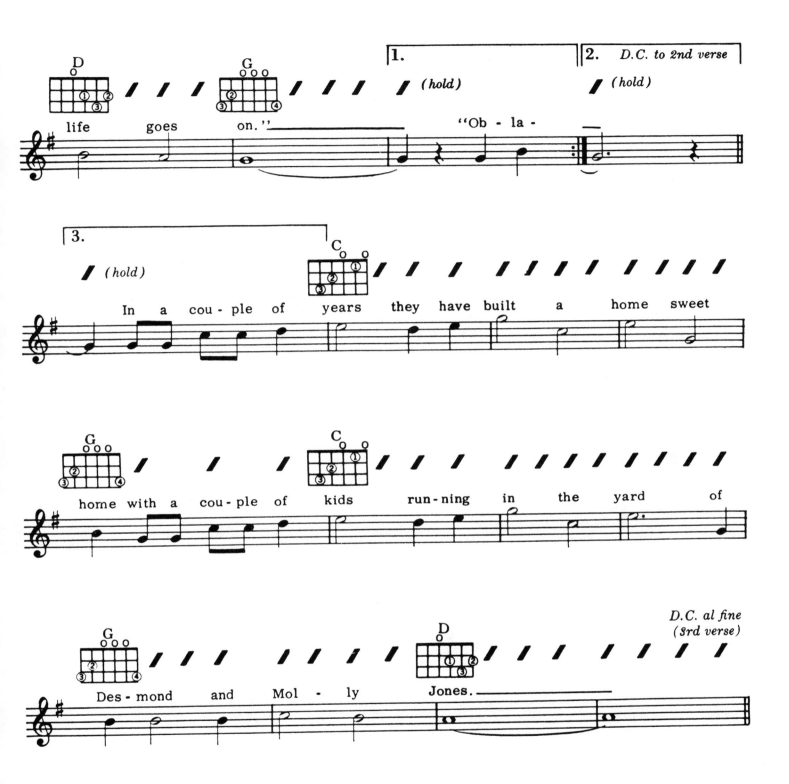

2. Desmond takes a trolley to the jeweller's store,
   Buys a twenty carat golden ring.
   Takes it back to Molly waiting at the door
   And as he gives it to her she begins to sing. (Chorus)

3. Happy ever after in the market place,
   Desmond lets the children lend a hand.
   Molly stays at home and does her pretty face
   And in the evening she still sings it with the band: (Chorus)

OH! DARLING

By JOHN LENNON and PAUL McCARTNEY

Starting note for singing:

Slowly

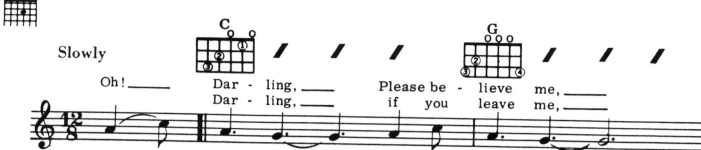

Oh! _____ Dar - ling, _____ Please be - lieve me, _____
Dar - ling, _____ if you leave me, _____

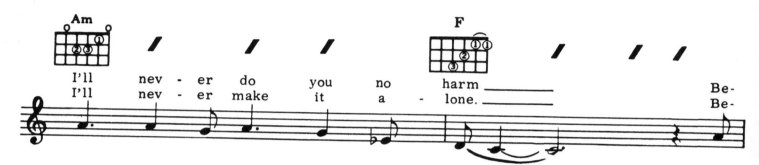

I'll nev - er do you no harm _____
I'll nev - er make it a - lone. _____ Be- Be-

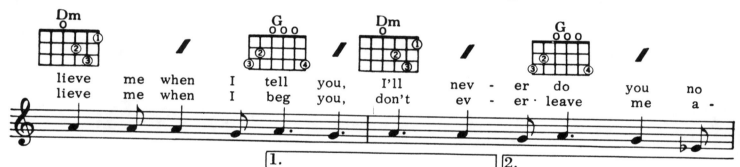

lieve me when I tell you, I'll nev - er do you no
lieve me when I beg you, don't ev - er leave me a -

1. | 2.

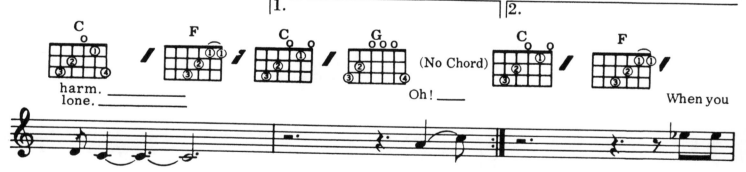

harm. _____
lone. _____ Oh! _____ When you

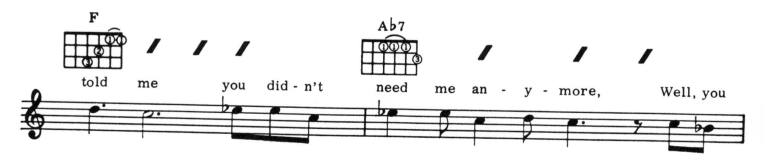

told me you did - n't need me an - y - more, Well, you

Oh! Darling, Please believe me,
I'll never let you down.
Believe me when I tell you,
I'll never do you no harm.

ONE AFTER 909

By JOHN LENNON and PAUL McCARTNEY

Repeat for additional verses

2. I begged her not to go and I begged her on my bended knees,
   You're only fooling around, you're only fooling around with me.
   I said move over once, move over twice,
   Come on, baby, don't be cold as ice.
   I said I'm trav'ling on the One After Nine-O-Nine.

3. Repeat first verse.

ONLY A NORTHERN SONG

By GEORGE HARRISON

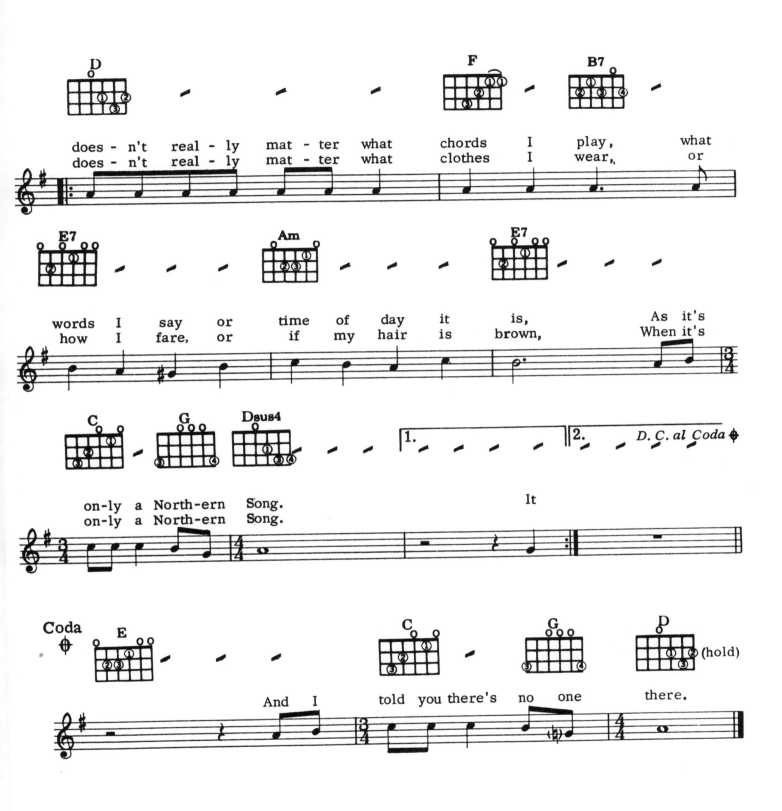

3. If you think the harmony
Is a little dark and out of key,
You're correct,
There's nobody there.

PAPERBACK WRITER

By JOHN LENNON and PAUL McCARTNEY

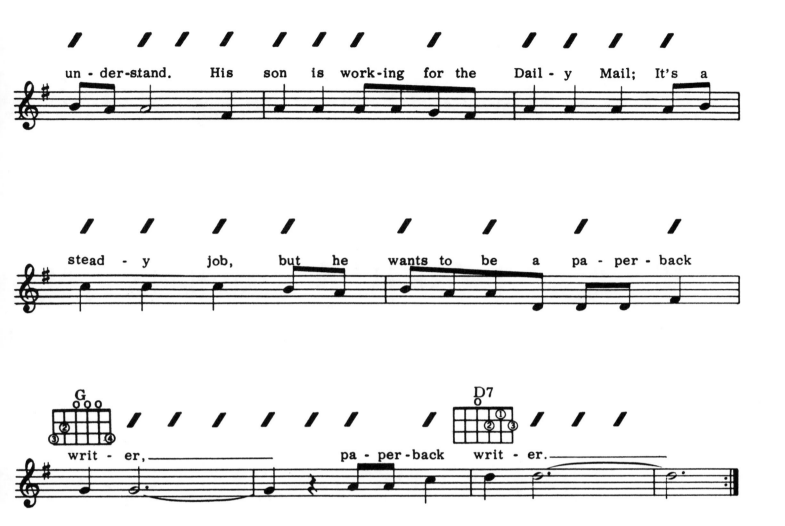

un - der-stand. His son is work-ing for the Dail - y Mail; It's a

stead - y job, but he wants to be a pa - per - back

G writ - er,_____ pa - per-back writ - er._____ **D7**

It's a thousand pages, give or take a few,
I'll be writing more in a week or two.
I can make it longer if you like the style,
I can change it 'round and I want to be a paperback writer, paperback writer.
If you really like it you can have the rights,
It could make a million for you overnight.
If you must return it you can send it here;
But I need a break and I want to be a paperback writer, paperback writer

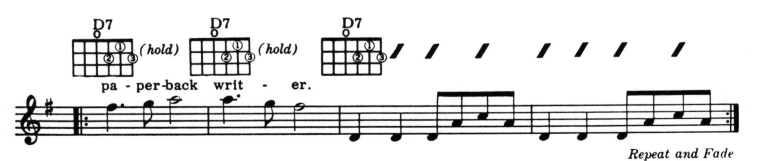

D7 *(hold)* **D7** *(hold)* **D7**
pa - per-back writ - er.

Repeat and Fade

PENNY LANE

By JOHN LENNON and PAUL McCARTNEY

Moderately Bright

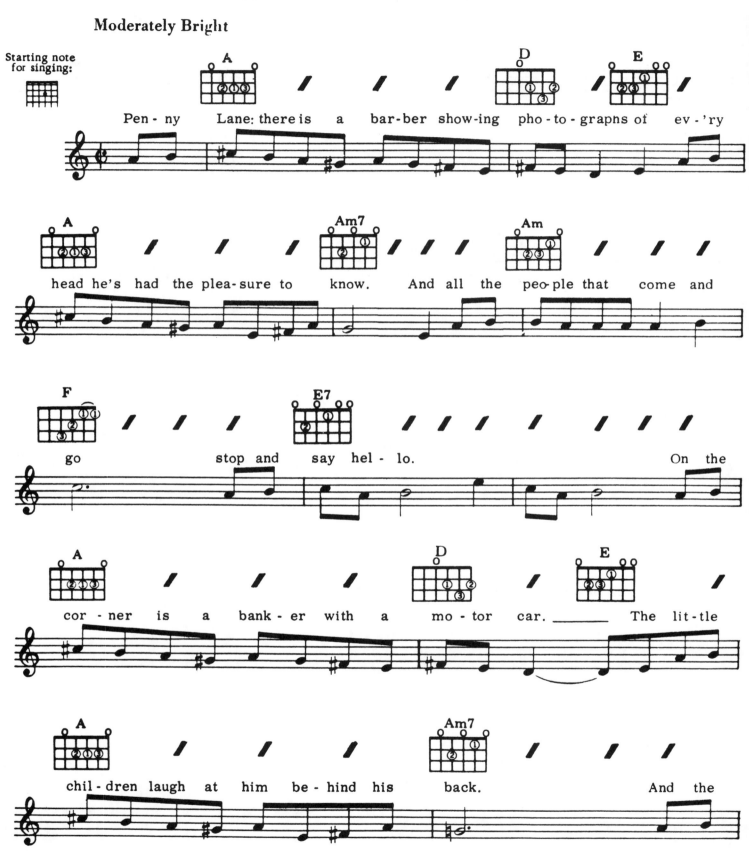

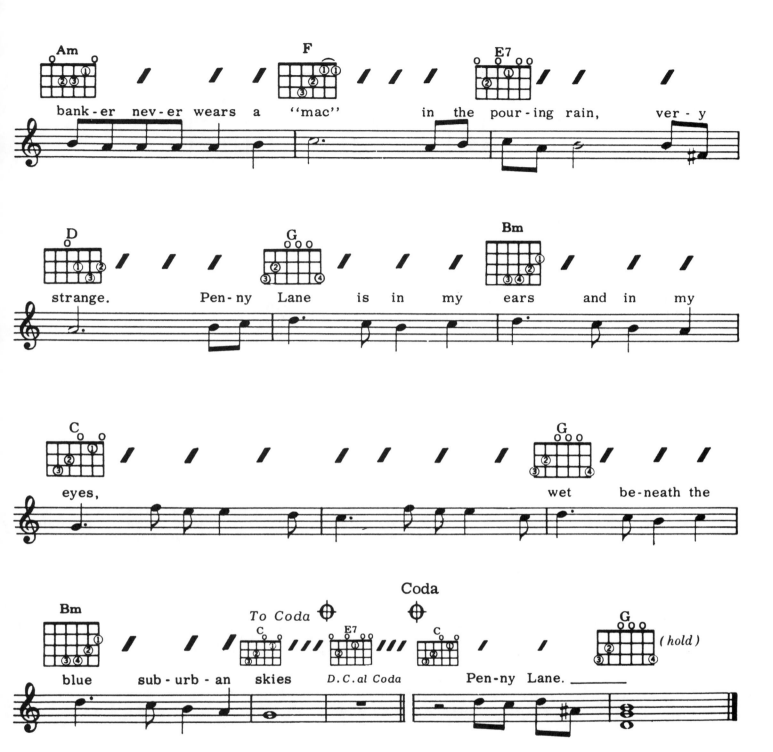

Back in Penny Lane: there is a fireman with an hourglass.
And in his pocket is a portrait of the queen.
He likes to keep his fire engine clean, it's a clean machine.
Penny Lane is in my ears and in my eyes.
Full of fish and finger pies in summer meanwhile

Back behind the shelter in the middle of the round-a-bout
A pretty nurse is selling poppies from a tray.
And tho' she feels as if she's in a play she is anyway.
Back in Penny Lane: the barber shaves another customer.
We see the banker sitting waiting for a trim.
And the the fireman rushes in from the pouring rain, very strange.

POLYTHENE PAM

By JOHN LENNON and PAUL McCARTNEY

RAIN

By JOHN LENNON and PAUL McCARTNEY

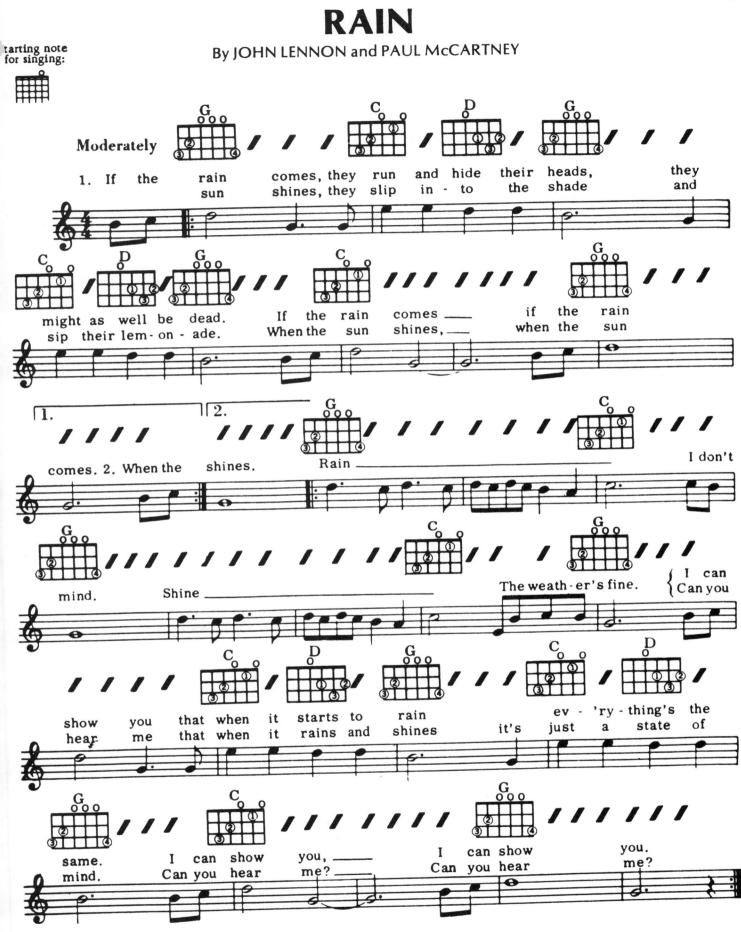

Moderately

1. If the rain comes, they run and hide their heads, they
   sun shines, they slip in-to the shade they and

might as well be dead. If the rain comes ____ if the rain
sip their lem-on-ade. When the rain shines, ____ when the sun

1.
comes. 2. When the shines.

2.
Rain ____ I don't

mind. Shine ____ The weath-er's fine. { I can
Can you

show you that when it starts to rain ev-'ry-thing's the
hear me that when it rains and shines it's just a state of

same. I can show you, ____ I can show you.
mind. Can you hear me? ____ Can you hear me?

REVOLUTION

By JOHN LENNON and PAUL McCARTNEY

Starting note for singing:

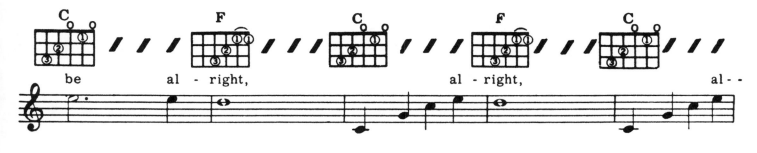

be al - right, al - right, al -

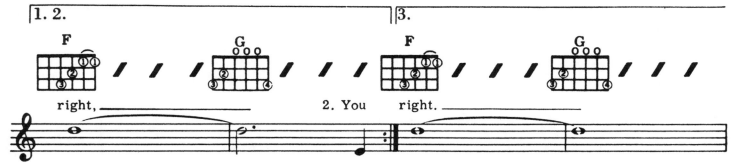

1. 2.

3.

right, _____ 2. You right. _____

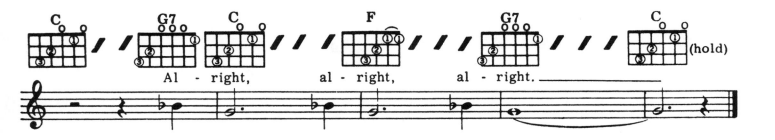

Al - right, al - right, al - right. _____ (hold)

2. You say you got a real solution,
 Well, you know, we'd all love to see the plan.
 You ask me for a contribution.
 Well, you know, We're all doing what we can.
 But if you want money for people with minds that hate,
 All I can tell you is,"Broth-er you have to wait."
 Don't you know it's gonna be alright, alright, alright,

3. You say you'll change the constitution,
 Well, you know, We all want to change your head.
 You tell me it's the institution.
 Well, you know, You better free your mind instead.
 But if you go carrying pictures of Chairman Mao,
 You ain't going to make it with anyone anyhow,
 Don't you know it's gonna be alright, alright, alright.

ROCKY RACCOON

By JOHN LENNON and PAUL McCARTNEY

Starting note
for singing:

Brightly, in 2 (♩=1 beat)

Am7   D7

Rock - y Rac - coon___ checked in - to his room___ were
she and her man___ who called him - self Dan___

G7   C   C/B

on - ly to find___ Gid-eon's Bi - ble.
in the next room___ at the hoe - down.

Am7   D7

Rock - y had come___ e - quipped with a gun___ to
Rock - y burst in___ and grin - ning a grin,___ He said,

G7   C   C/B

shoot off the legs___ of his ri - val. His
"Dan - ny boy, this___ is a show - down." But

Am7   D7

ri - val it seems___ had bro - ken his dreams___ by
Dan - iel was hot,___ he drew first and shot___ and

G7   C   C/B

steal - ing the girl___ of his fan - cy. Her
Rock - y col - lapsed___ in the cor - ner. *(continue as guitar solo)*

Am7 / / / / / / / **D7** / / /
name was Ma - gill,_____ But she called her - self Lil,_____

G7 / / / / / / / / /
_____ But ev - 'ry - one knew_____ her as Nan-

1. **C** / / / **C/B** / / / **2.** **C** / / / **C/B** / / /
- cy. Now Now the

Am7 / / / / / **D7** / / / / /
doc - tor came in_____ stink - ing of gin_____ and pro-
Rock - y Rac - coon,_____ he fell back in his room_____

G7 / / / / / **C** / / / **C/B** / / /
ceed - ed to lie_____ on the ta - ble. He said,
on - ly to find_____ Gid - eon's Bi - ble.

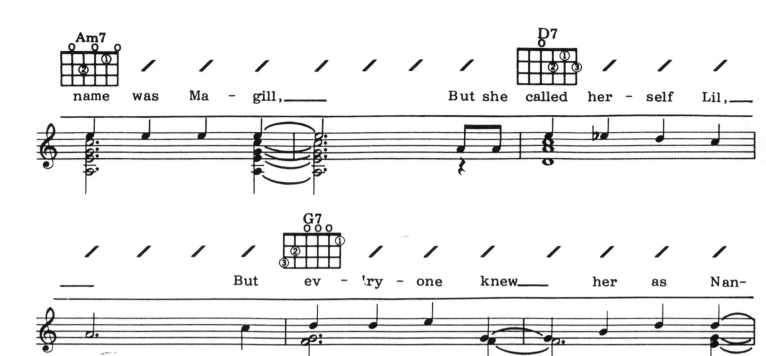
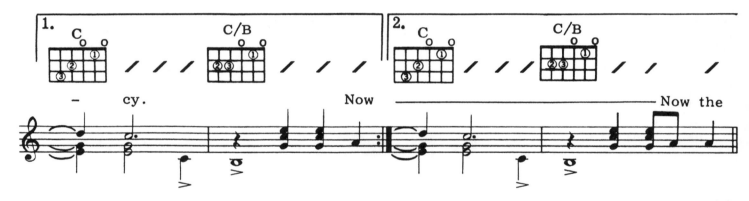
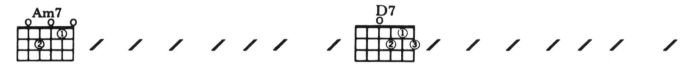
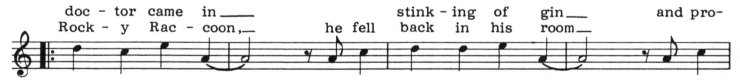
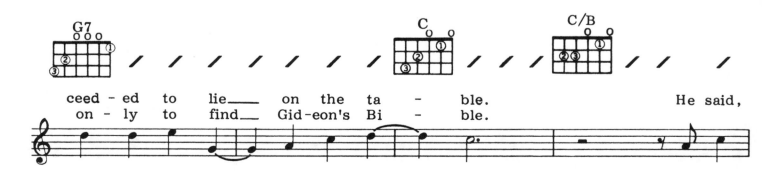

"Rock-y, you met___ your match," And Rock-y said, "Doc, it's on-ly a
Gid - eon checked out___ And he___ left it no doubt

scratch, And I'll be bet-ter, I'll be bet-ter Doc, as soon___ as I'm
To help with good Rock - y's re - vi -

1. a - ble." Now **2.** - val.

RUN FOR YOUR LIFE

By JOHN LENNON and PAUL McCARTNEY

D7
can, lit - tle girl.

Am7
Hide your head in the

D7
sand, lit - tle girl.

Am
Catch you with an - oth - er

F **E7** **Am**
man that's the end, ah, lit - tle girl.

C7

(Guitar)

1.2.3.
C7

4.
C7

Repeat and fade

2. Well, you   No no no.   No no

3. Let this be a sermon.
   I mean everything I said.
   Baby, I'm determined,
   And I'd rather see you dead.

   Chorus

4. I'd rather see you dead, little girl,
   Than to be with another man.
   You'd better keep your head, little girl,
   Or I won't know where I am.

   Chorus

SEXY SADIE

By JOHN LENNON and PAUL McCARTNEY

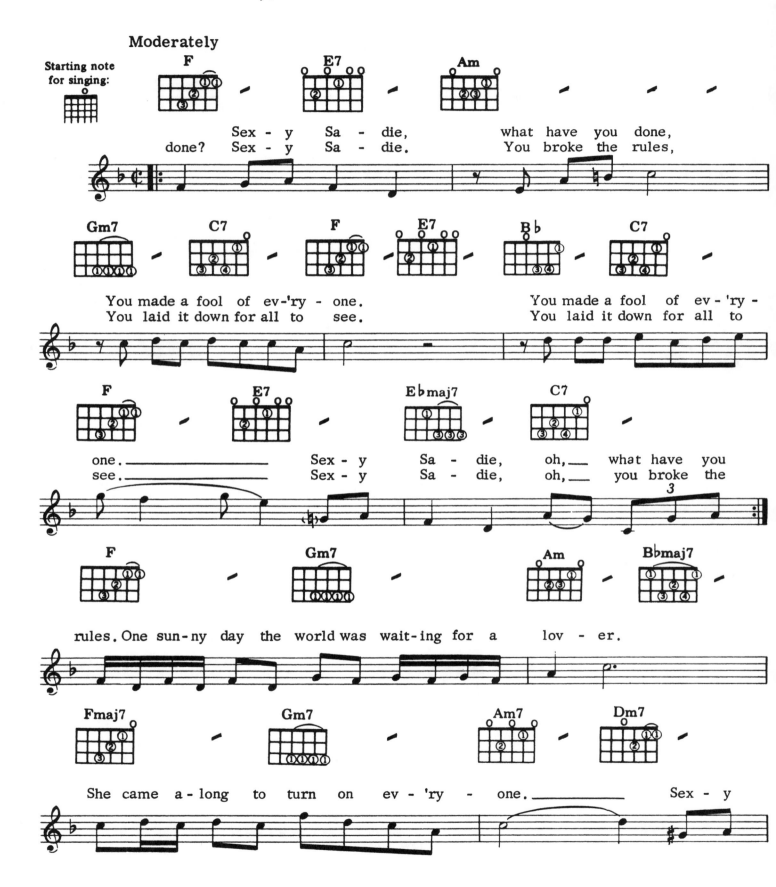

225

SGT. PEPPER'S LONELY HEARTS CLUB BAND

By JOHN LENNON and PAUL McCARTNEY

Chorus

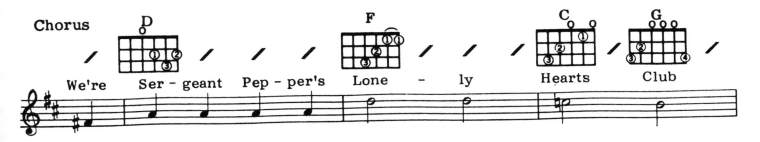

We're Ser-geant Pep-per's Lone-ly Hearts Club

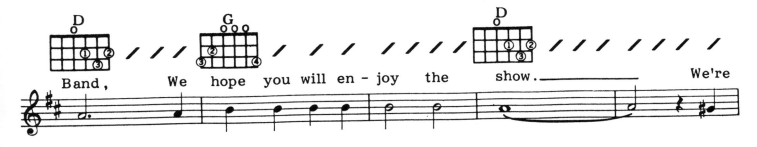

Band, We hope you will en-joy the show._____ We're

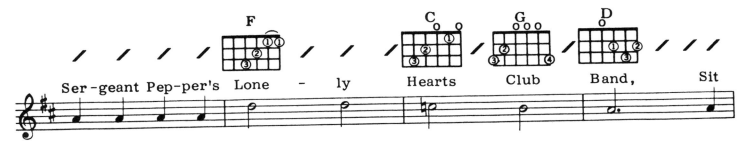

Ser-geant Pep-per's Lone-ly Hearts Club Band, Sit

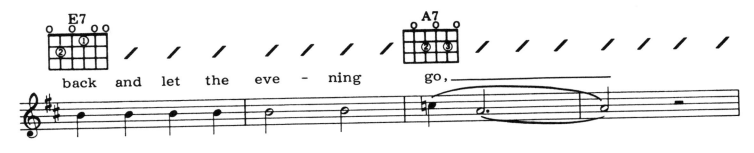

back and let the eve-ning go,_____

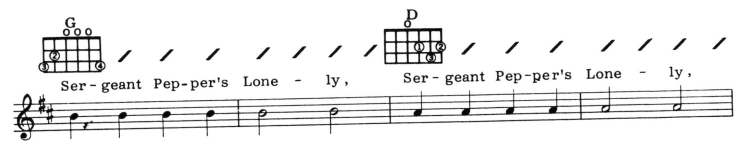

Ser-geant Pep-per's Lone-ly, Ser-geant Pep-per's Lone-ly,

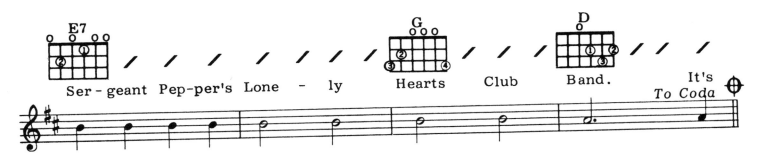

Ser-geant Pep-per's Lone-ly Hearts Club Band. It's
To Coda

228

G   C7

won - der - ful to be here, it's cer - tain - ly a thrill, You're

G   A7

such a love - ly au - di - ence, we'd like to take you

(hold)

home with us, we'd love to take you home.

D.C. al Coda

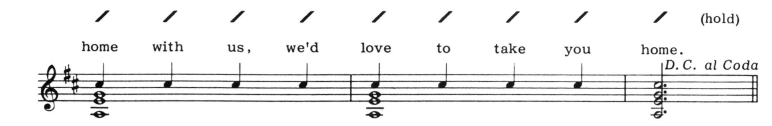

Coda

D   F   C   G

Ser - geant Pep - per's Lone - ly Hearts Club

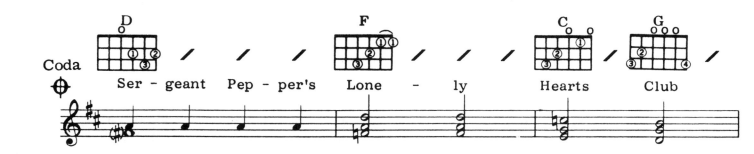

D   G   D

Band, We'd like to thank you once a - gain._____

SHE CAME IN THROUGH THE BATHROOM WINDOW

By JOHN LENNON and PAUL McCARTNEY

Starting note for singing:

Moderately Slow

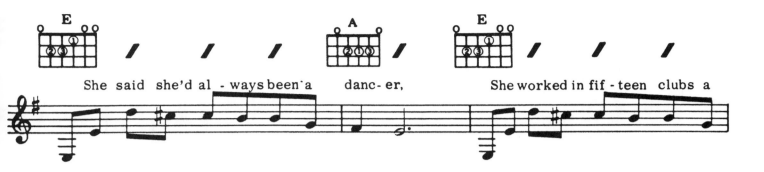

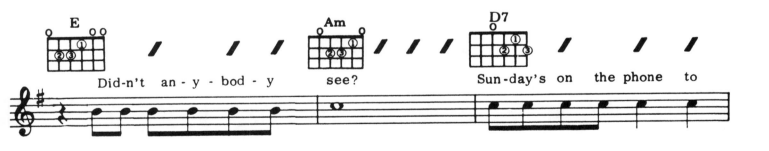

D.C. al Fine

SHE SAID SHE SAID

By JOHN LENNON and PAUL McCARTNEY

Moderately

Starting note for singing:

1. She said _____ I know what it's like to be dead,
2. I said _____ who put all those things in your hair,

I know what it is to be sad.
Things that make me feel that I'm mad.

And she's
And you're

mak-ing me feel like I've nev-er been born. *Guitar*

1.

2.

She said you don't un-der-

stand what I said, I said; No, no, no, you're wrong, when I was a

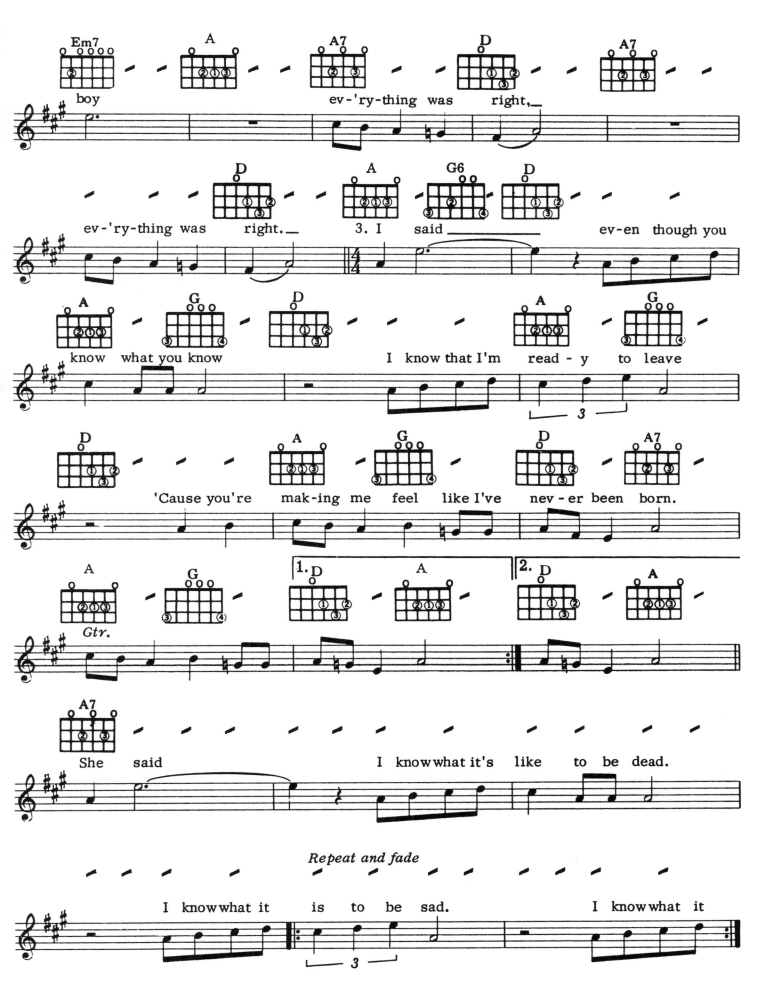

SHE'S A WOMAN

By JOHN LENNON and PAUL McCARTNEY

A7   E7

Turn me on when I get lone - ly,
She will nev - er make me jeal - ous,

D7   A7   D7

Peo - ple tell me that she's on - ly fool - in', I know she is-n't.
Gives me all her time as well as lov - in', don't ask me why.

A7   C#m 4 fr. (hold)   F# (hold)

She's a wom-an who un - der - stands,

D.S. 𝄋

C#m 4 fr. (hold)   D   E   A7   *Repeat and fade*

She's a wom-an who loves her man;

SHE'S LEAVING HOME

By JOHN LENNON and PAUL McCARTNEY

Starting note
for singing:

Moderately

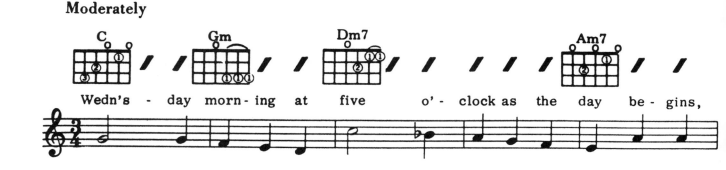

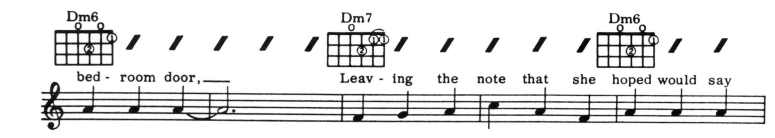

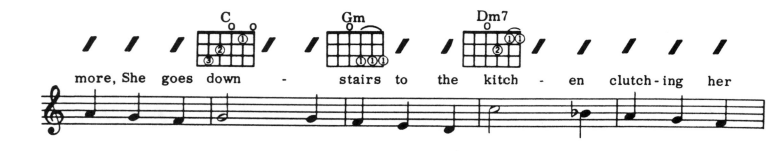

2. Father snores as his wife gets into her dressing gown,
   Picks up the letter that's lying there
   Standing alone at the top of the stairs
   She breaks down and cries to her husband,
   "Daddy, our baby's gone!
   Why would she treat us so thoughtlessly
   How could she do this to me?"
   She (We never thought of ourselves) is leaving (Never thought for ourselves)
   Home (We struggled hard all our lives to get by)
   She's leaving home after living alone for so many years. (Bye, bye.)

3. Friday morning at nine o'clock she is far away
   Waiting to keep the appointment she made
   Meeting a man from the motor trade.
   She (What did we do that was wrong) is having (We didn't know it was wrong)
   Fun (Fun is the one thing that money can't buy)
   Something inside that was always denied for so many years.
   (Then to final ending)

STRAWBERRY FIELDS FOREVER

By JOHN LENNON and PAUL McCARTNEY

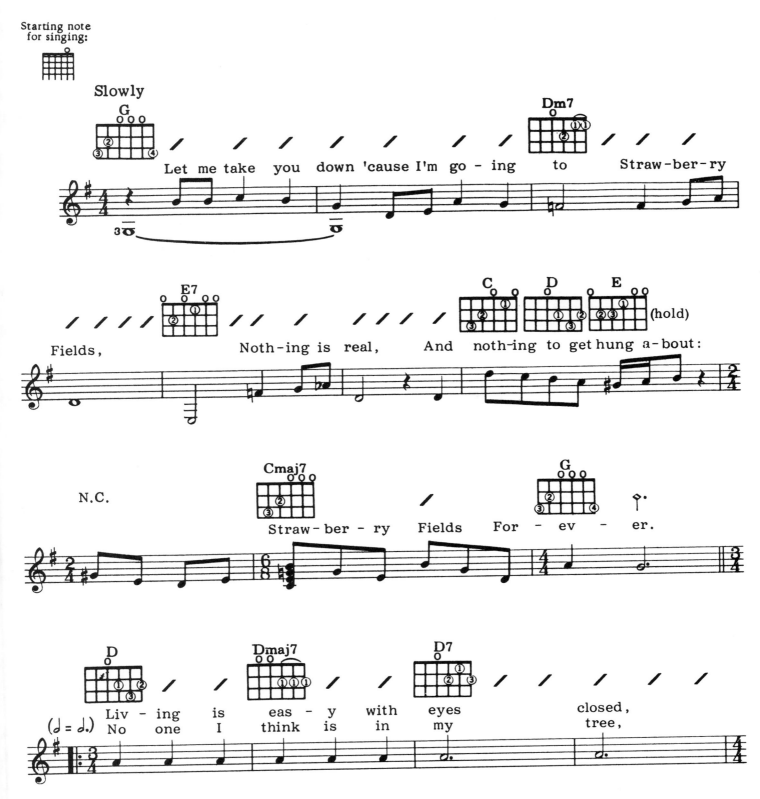

Mis - un - der - stand - ing all you see.
I mean it must be high or low.

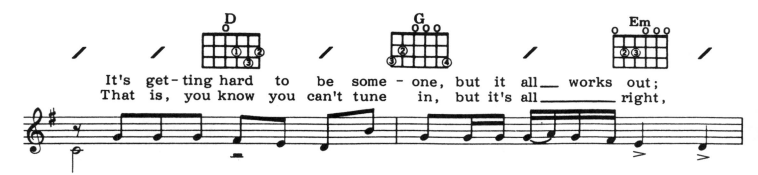

It's get-ting hard to be some - one, but it all__ works out;
That is, you know you can't tune in, but it's all_____ right,

it does - n't mat - ter much to me.
that is, I think it's much not too bad.

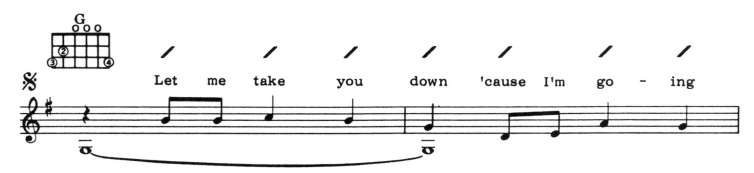

Let me take you down 'cause I'm go - ing

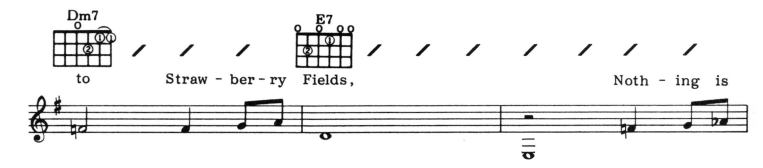

to Straw - ber - ry Fields, Noth - ing is

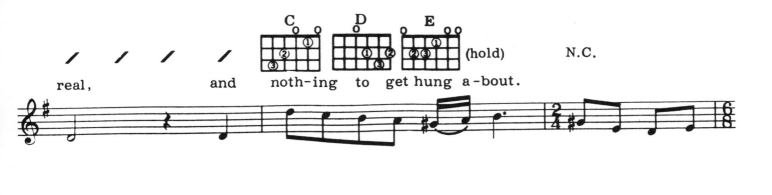

real, and noth-ing to get hung a-bout.

Straw-ber-ry Fields For - ev - er.

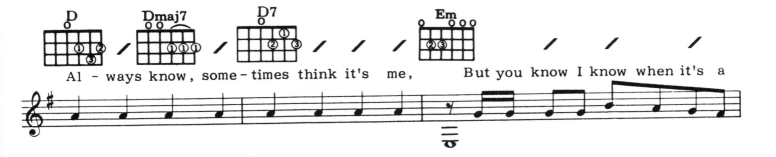

Al - ways know, some-times think it's me, But you know I know when it's a

dream. I think I know I mean a "Yes" but it's all wrong,

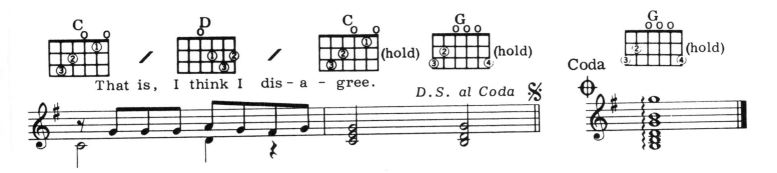

That is, I think I dis-a - gree.

SUN KING

By JOHN LENNON and PAUL McCARTNEY

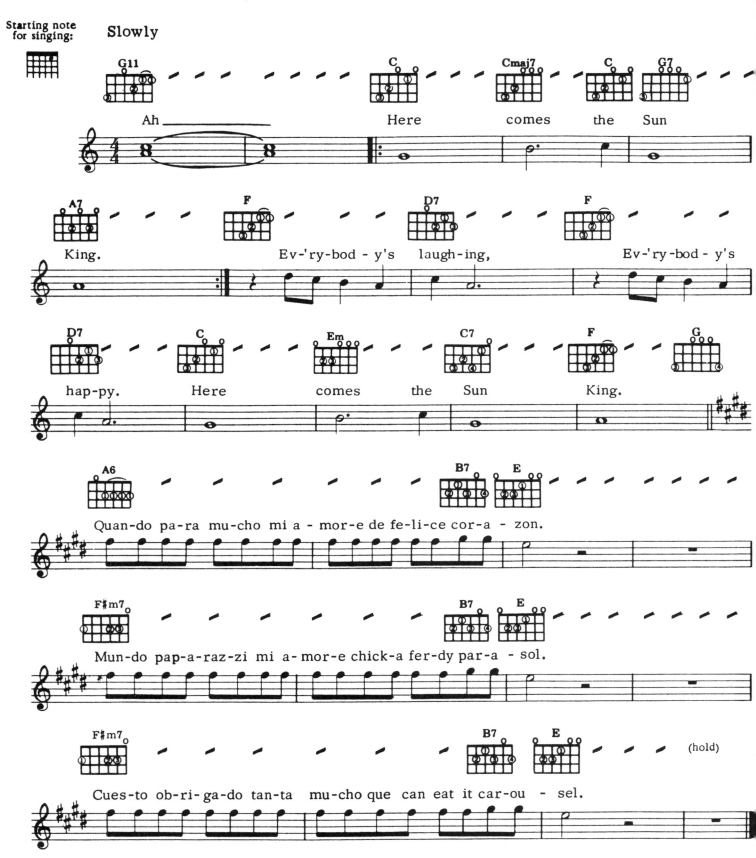

TELL ME WHAT YOU SEE

By JOHN LENNON and PAUL McCARTNEY

Starting note
for singing:

Moderately

If you let me take your heart, I will prove to you,

We will nev-er be a-part If I'm part of you.

O-pen up your eyes, now, Tell me what you see,

It is no sur-prise, now, what you see is me.

Dm6 *Interlude and final ending* Tell me what you see. *(hold)*

Big and black the clouds may be, time will pass away.
If you put your trust in me, I'll make bright your day.
Look into these eyes, now, tell me what you see,
Don't you realize, now, what you see is me.
(to Interlude)

Listen to me one more time, how can I get through?
Can't you try to see that I'm tryin' to get to you?
Open up your eyes, now, tell me what you see.
It is no surprise now, what you see is me.
(to Final Ending)

TAXMAN

By GEORGE HARRISON

3. Don't ask me what I want it for,
   If you don't want to pay some more.
   'Cause I'm the taxman,
   Yeh, I'm the taxman.

4. Now my advice for those who die:
   Beware the pennies on your eye!
   'Cause I'm the taxman,
   Yeh, I'm the taxman,
   And you're working for no one but me.

TELL ME WHY

By JOHN LENNON and PAUL McCARTNEY

Starting note
for singing:

Moderately

Tell me why _____ you cried, And why you lied _____ to me. __ Tell me why _____ you cried, And why you lied _____ to me.

1.2.

Well, I gave you ev-'ry-thing I had ____ But you
If it's some-thing that I've said or done ____ Tell me

left me sit-ting on my own. Did you have to treat me oh, so
what and I'll ap-ol-o-gize. If you don't, I real-ly can't go

Starting note
for singing:

THANK YOU GIRL

By JOHN LENNON and PAUL McCARTNEY

Moderately bright, with a beat

THINGS WE SAID TODAY

By JOHN LENNON and PAUL McCARTNEY

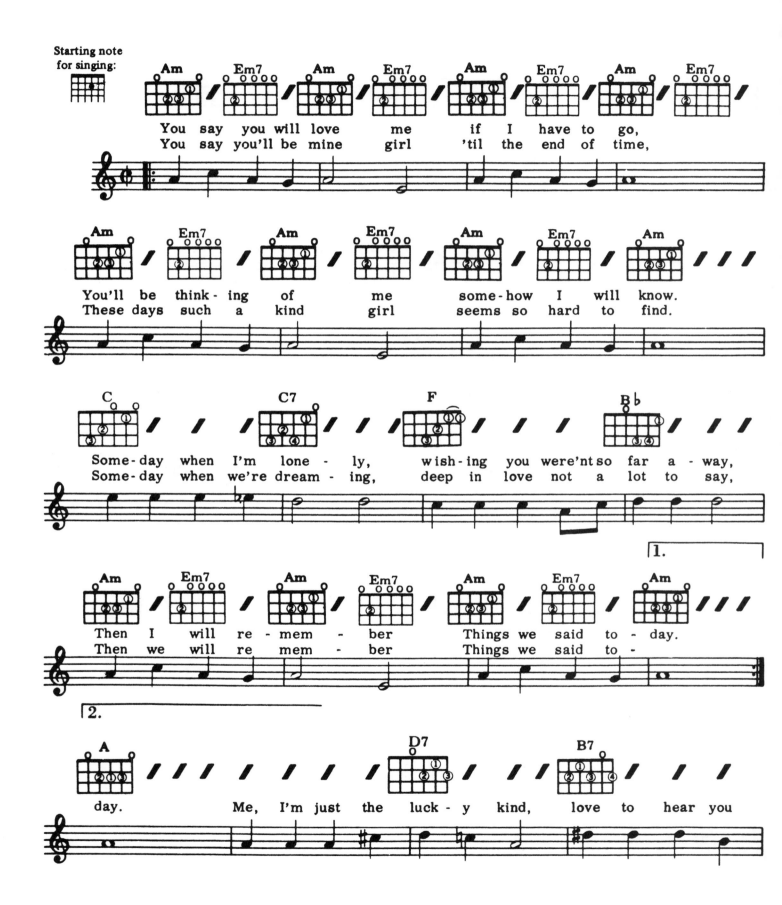

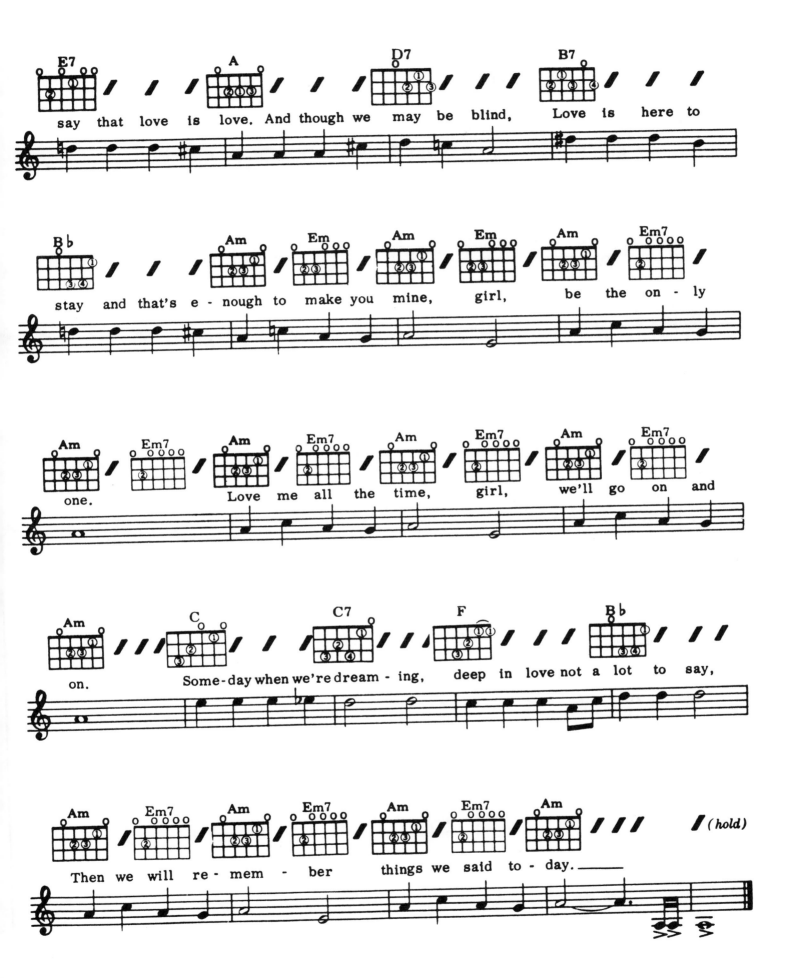

THINK FOR YOURSELF

By GEORGE HARRISON

Starting note for singing:

Moderately

1. I've got a word or two to say a-
2. I left you word far be-hind the ru-ins

bout the things that you do.
of the life that you had in mind.

You're tell-ing
And though you

all those lies
still can't see,

a - bout the
I know your

good things that we
mind's made up, you're

can have if we close our eyes.}
gon - na cause more mis - er - y.

Do what you want to

do, and go where you're go - ing to.

3. Although your mind's opaque
   Try thinking more if just for your own sake.
   The future still looks good
   And you've got time to rectify all the things that you should.

THIS BOY (Ringo's Theme)

By JOHN LENNON and PAUL McCARTNEY

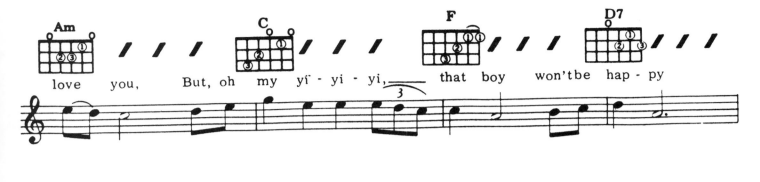

love you, But, oh my yï - yi - yi,___ that boy won't be hap - py

Till he's seen you cry hi - hi - hi.___ This boy

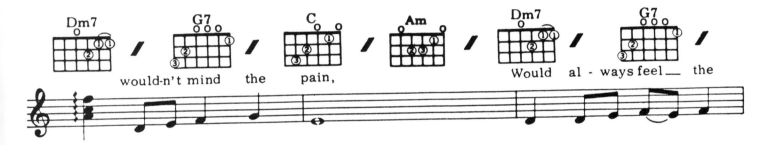

would-n't mind the pain, Would al - ways feel___ the

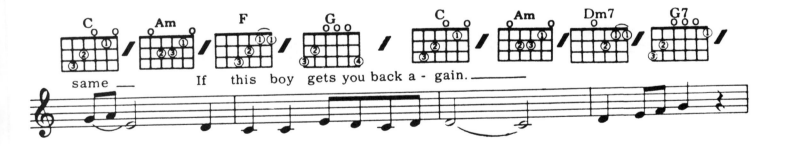

same ___ If this boy gets you back a - gain. _____

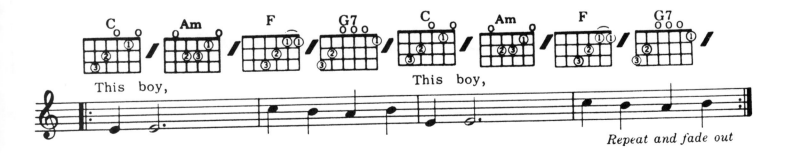

This boy, This boy,

Repeat and fade out

TICKET TO RIDE

By JOHN LENNON and PAUL McCARTNEY

TOMORROW NEVER KNOWS

By JOHN LENNON and PAUL McCARTNEY

Starting note
for singing:

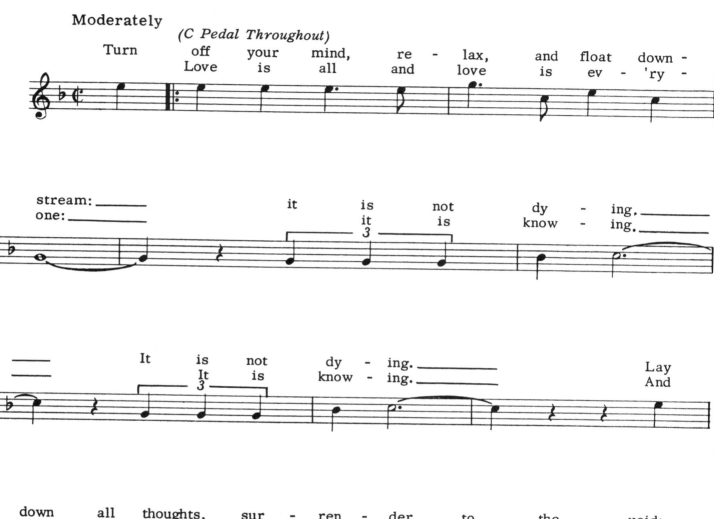

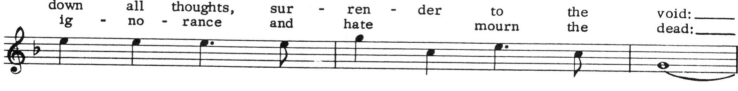

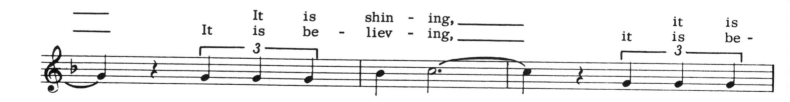

TWO OF US

By JOHN LENNON and PAUL McCARTNEY

Starting note
for singing:

Fairly bright, in 2

1. Two of us rid - ing no - where, spend - ing
2. Two of us send - ing post-cards, writ - ing

some-one's hard - earned pay;
let - ters hard on my wall;

You and me Sun - day driv - ing, not ar -
You and me burn - ing match-es, lift - ing

riv - ing on our way back
latch - es on our way back

home. }
home. } We're on our way home,

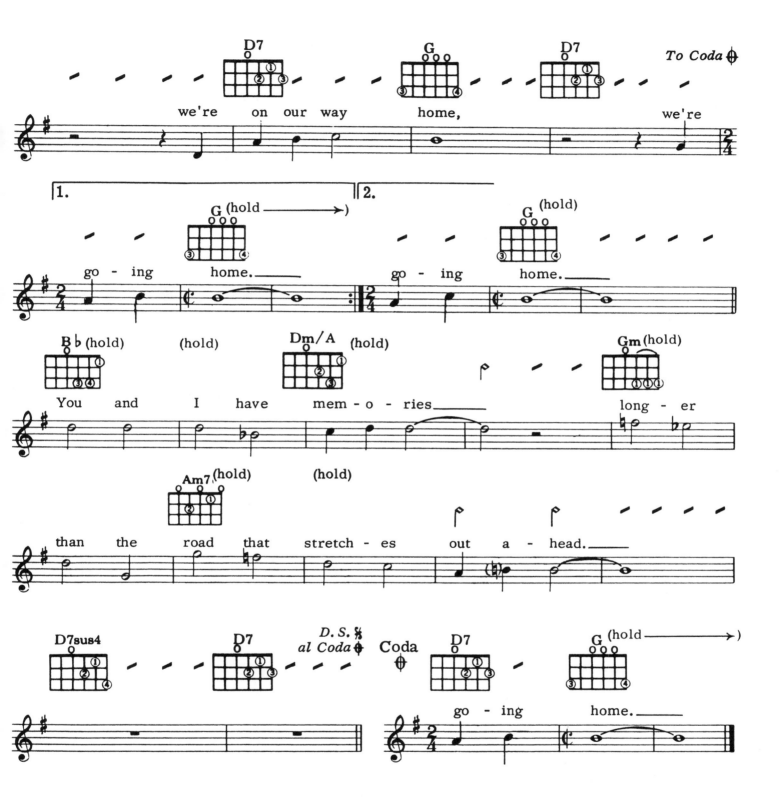

3. Two of us wearing raincoats, standing solo in the sun;
   You and me chasing paper, getting nowhere, on our way back home.
   We're on our way home, we're on our way home, We're *to Coda*

WAIT

By JOHN LENNON and PAUL McCARTNEY

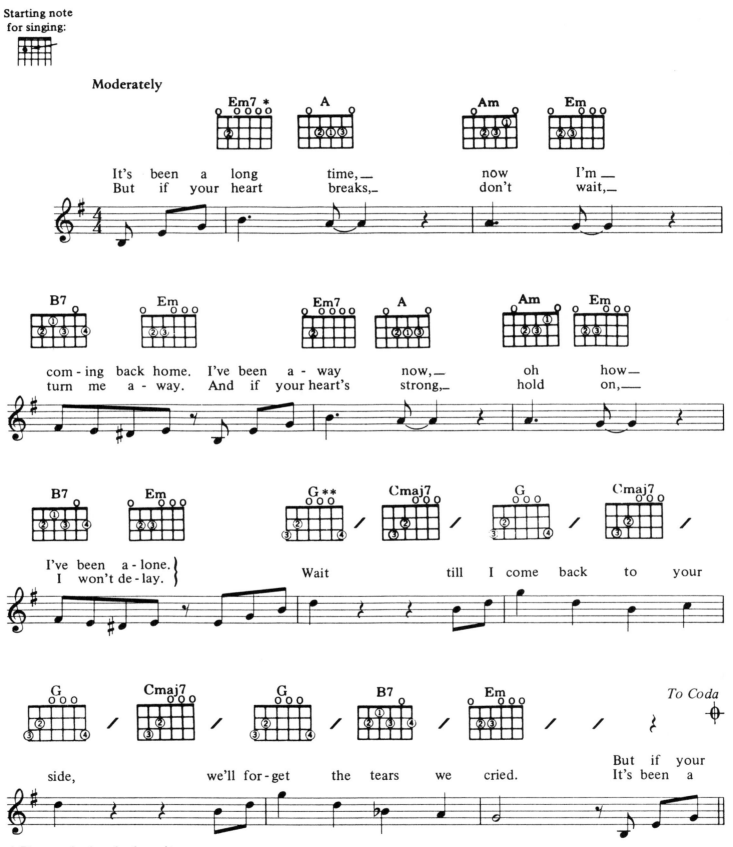

* Play each chord where it appears
** Steady beat

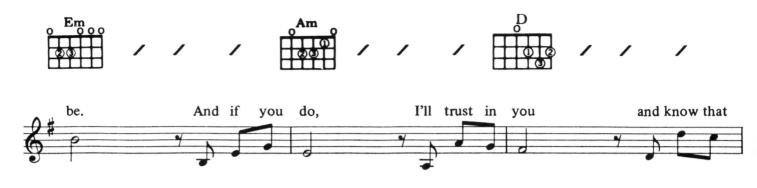

be.　　　And if you do,　　I'll trust in you　　　and know that

you　　　will wait for　me. _____ It's been a　　me _____ *D.C. al Coda*

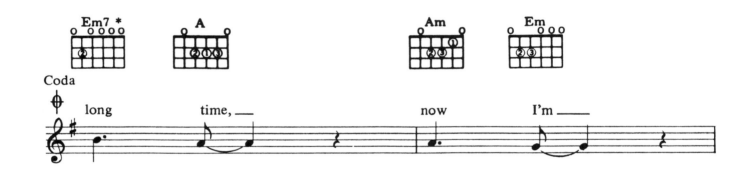

Coda

long　　　time, ___　　　　　now　I'm ___

com - ing back home.　I've been a - way　　now, ___

oh　　how___　　　I've been　a - lone.

slower

WHAT YOU'RE DOING

By JOHN LENNON and PAUL McCARTNEY

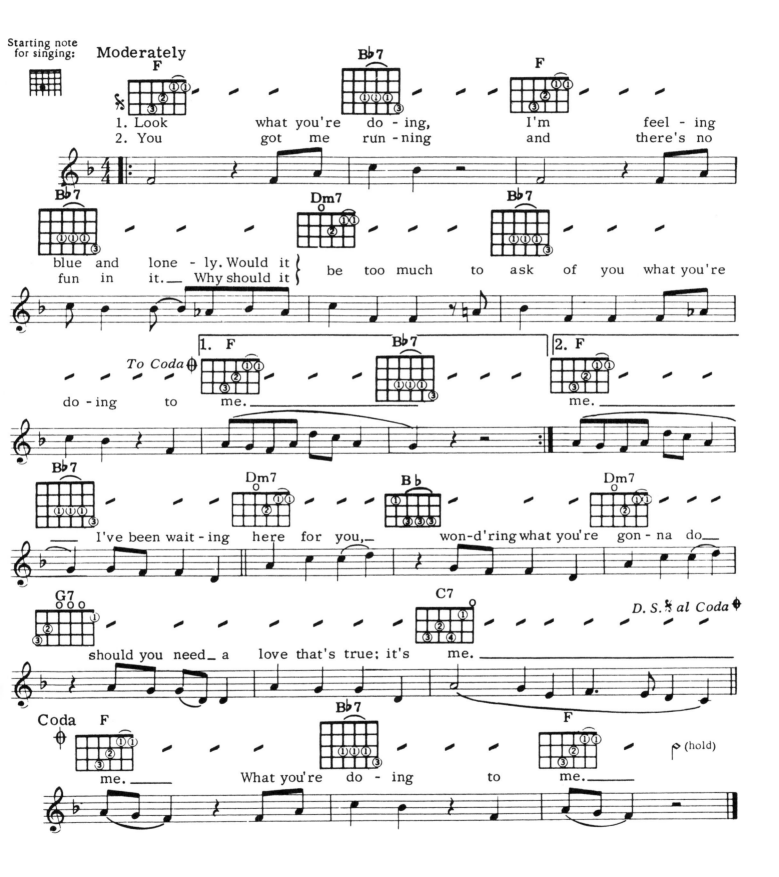

WE CAN WORK IT OUT

By JOHN LENNON and PAUL McCARTNEY

Starting note for singing:

Moderately Slow

WHAT GOES ON

By JOHN LENNON, PAUL McCARTNEY and RICHARD STARKEY

Starting note
for singing:

Moderately

What goes ‰ on _____ in your heart, What goes

on _____ in your mind? You are

tear - ing me a - part When you

treat _____ me so un - kind. What goes

on _____ in your mind? 1. The

3. I used to think of no one else but you were just the same,
   You didn't even think of me as someone with a name.
   Did you mean to break my heart and watch me die,
   Tell me why.
   What goes on in your heart, *(etc.)*

WHEN I GET HOME

By JOHN LENNON and PAUL McCARTNEY

Starting note
for singing:

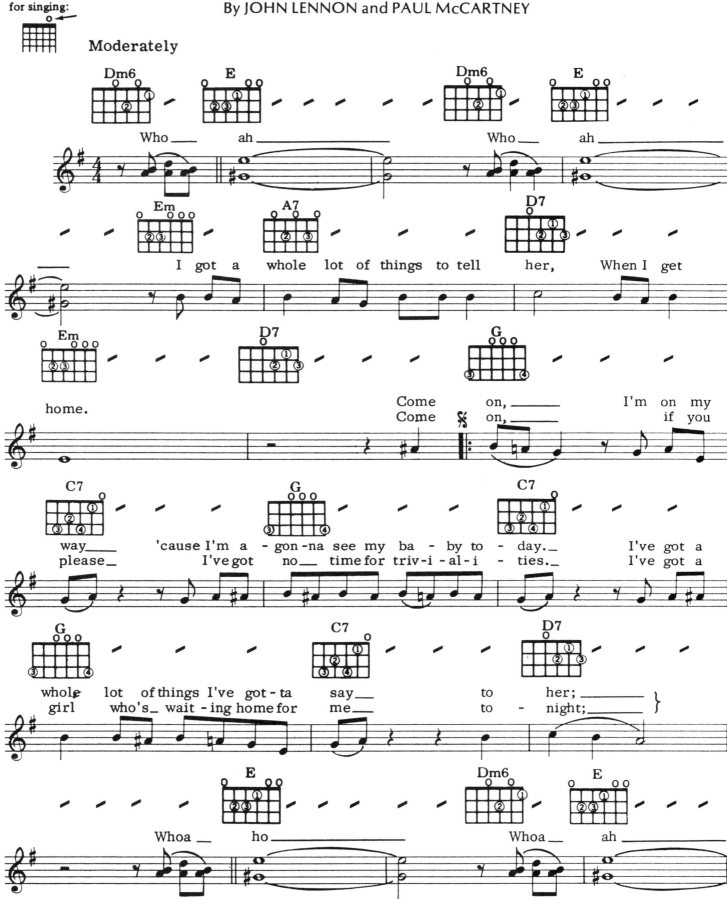

3. Come on, let me through.
   I've got so many things I've got to do.
   I've got no bus'ness being here with you this way;
   Whoa ho, Whoa ah *(etc.)*

WHEN I'M SIXTY FOUR

By JOHN LENNON and PAUL McCARTNEY

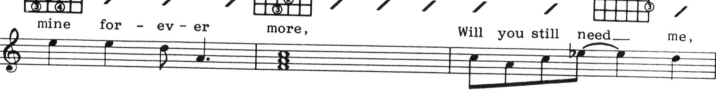

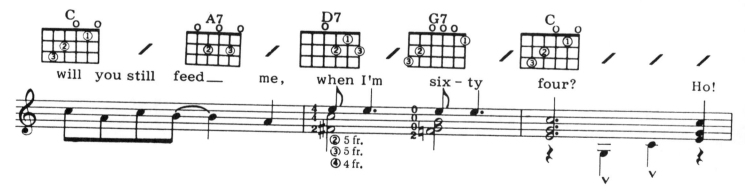

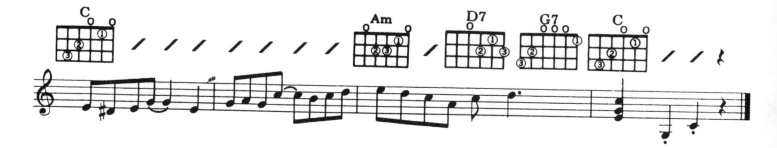

WHY DON'T WE DO IT IN THE ROAD

By JOHN LENNON and PAUL McCARTNEY

WITH A LITTLE HELP FROM MY FRIENDS

By JOHN LENNON and PAUL McCARTNEY

Starting note
for singing:

THE WORD

By JOHN LENNON and PAUL McCARTNEY

3. Say the word and you'll be free,
   Say the word and be like me.
   Say the word I'm thinking of.
   Have you heard the word is love?
   It's so fine, it's sunshine,
   It's the word love.
   Now that I know what I feel must be right,
   I mean to show ev'rybody the light.

4. Give the word a chance to say
   That the word is just the way.
   It's the word I'm thinking of
   And the only word is love.
   It's so fine, it's sunshine,
   It's the word love.
   Say the word love. Say the word love.

YELLOW SUBMARINE

By JOHN LENNON and PAUL McCARTNEY

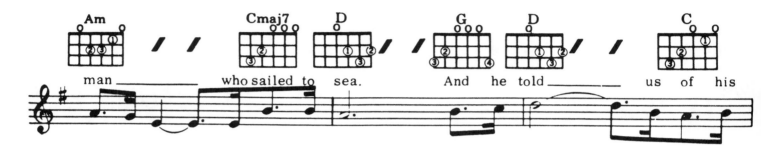

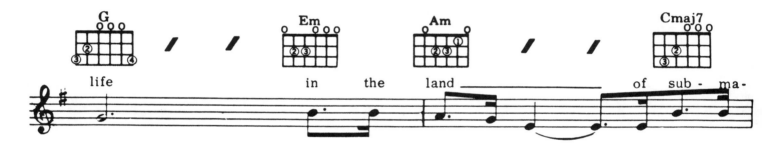

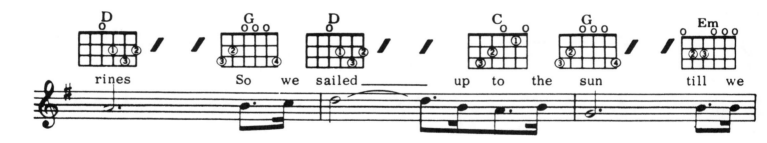

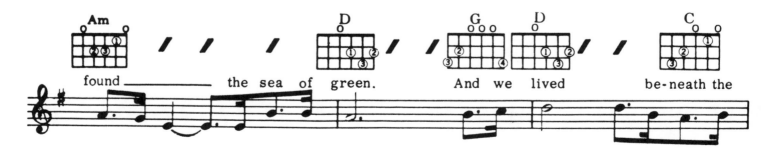

So we sailed up to the sun,
Till we found the sea of green,
And we lived beneath the waves,
In our Yellow Submarine. (Cho.)

And our friends are all aboard,
Many more of them live next door,
And the band begins to play. (Inst.)
(Chorus)

As we live a life of ease,
Everyone of us has all we need,
Sky of blue and sea of green,
In our Yellow Submarine. (Cho.)

YER BLUES

By JOHN LENNON and PAUL McCARTNEY

Starting note
for singing:

Slow Blues

Yes, I'm lone - ly, (Guitar)

Wan - na die. Gtr.

Yes, I'm lone - ly, (Gtr.)

Wan - na die. (Gtr.)

If I ain't dead al - read - y.

3. The black cloud crossed my mind,
   Blue mist 'round my soul.
   I feel so suicidal,
   Even hate my rock and roll.

YES IT IS

By JOHN LENNON and PAUL McCARTNEY

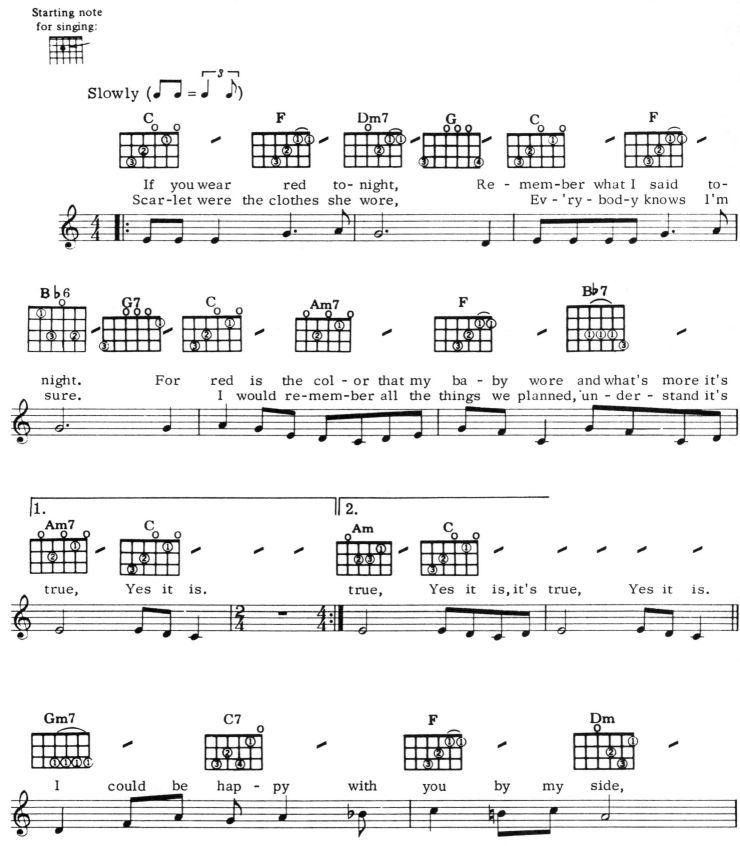

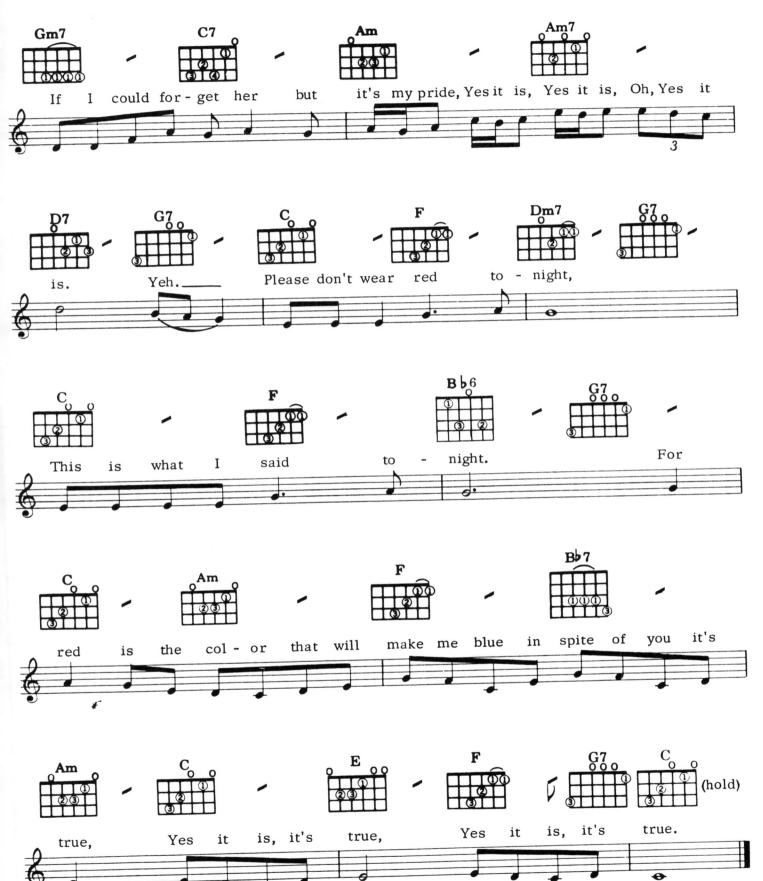

YESTERDAY

By JOHN LENNON and PAUL McCARTNEY

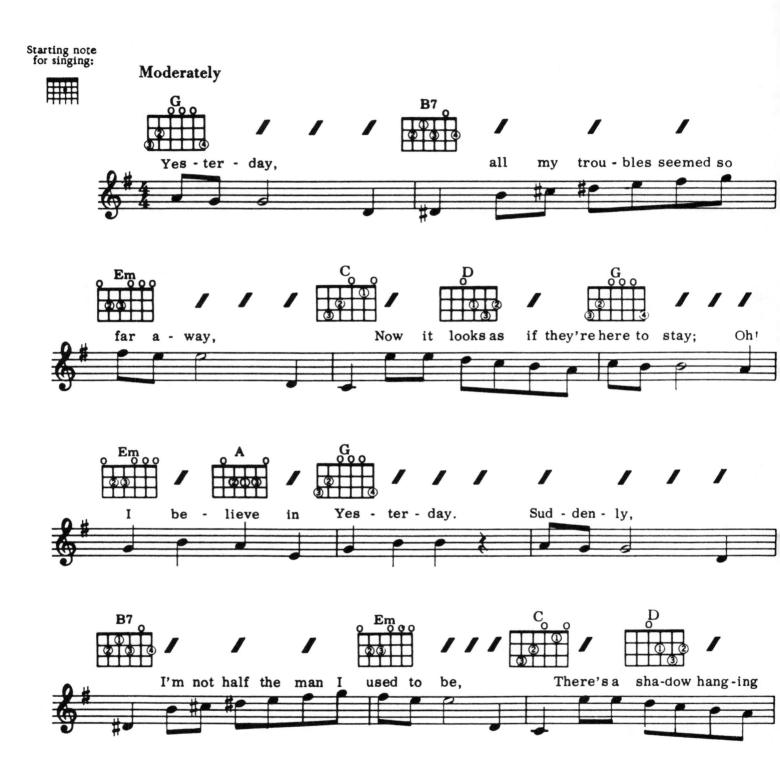

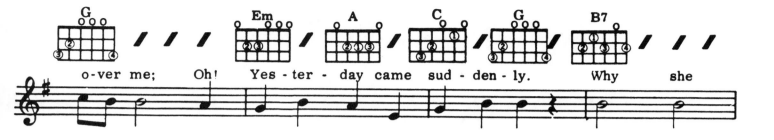

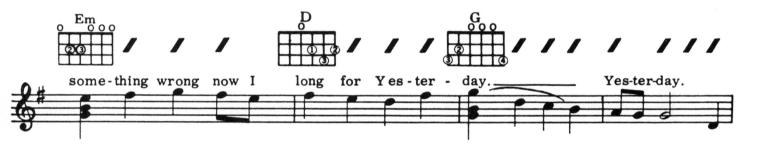

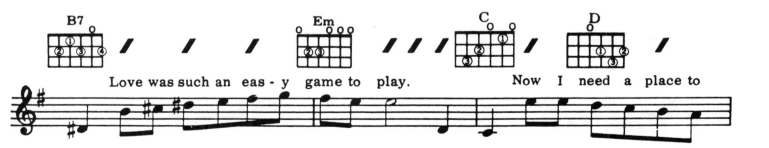

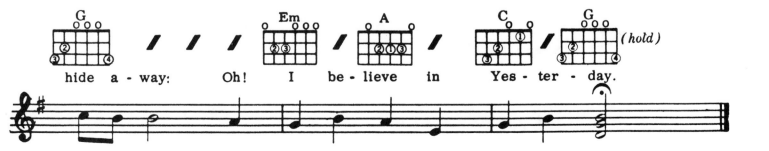

YOU CAN'T DO THAT

By JOHN LENNON and PAUL McCARTNEY

Starting note
for singing:

Moderately

D7   D7sus4   D7

1. I got some - thing to say that might cause you pain; If I
sec-ond time I've caught you talk-ing to him. Do I

D7sus4   D7

catch you talk - ing to that boy a - gain, I'm gon - na
have to tell you one more time I think it's a sin? I think I'll

G7

let you down _____ and leave you

D7   A7

flat, _____ Be-cause I've told you be - fore,

3. (So,) please listen to me if you wanna stay mine.
   I can't help my feelings, I'll go out of my mind.
   I'm gonna let you down and leave you flat,
   Because I've told you before, oh you can't do that.

YOU KNOW MY NAME
(Look Up The Number)

By JOHN LENNON and PAUL McCARTNEY

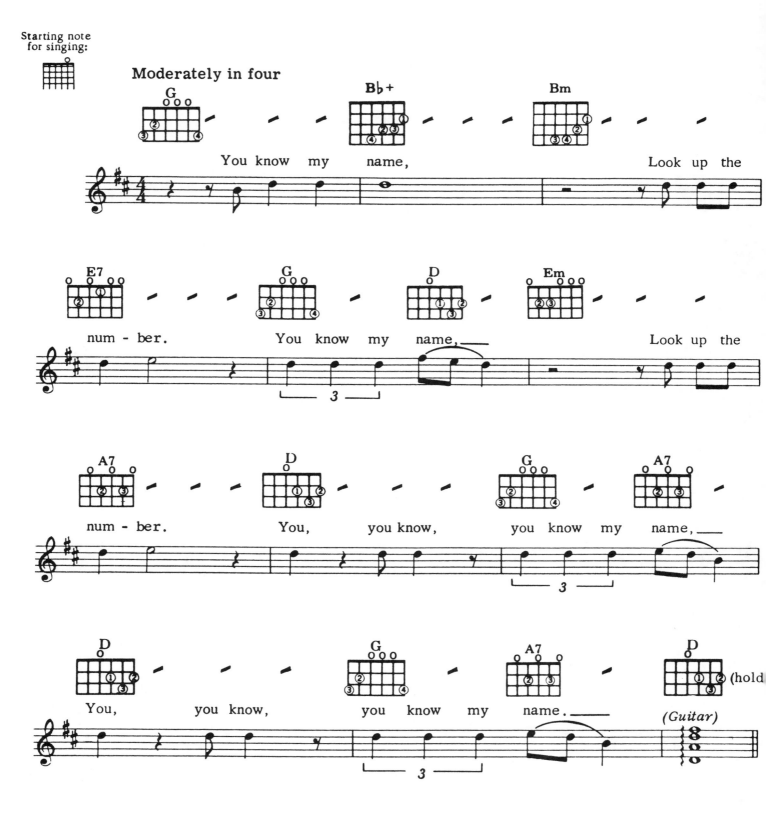

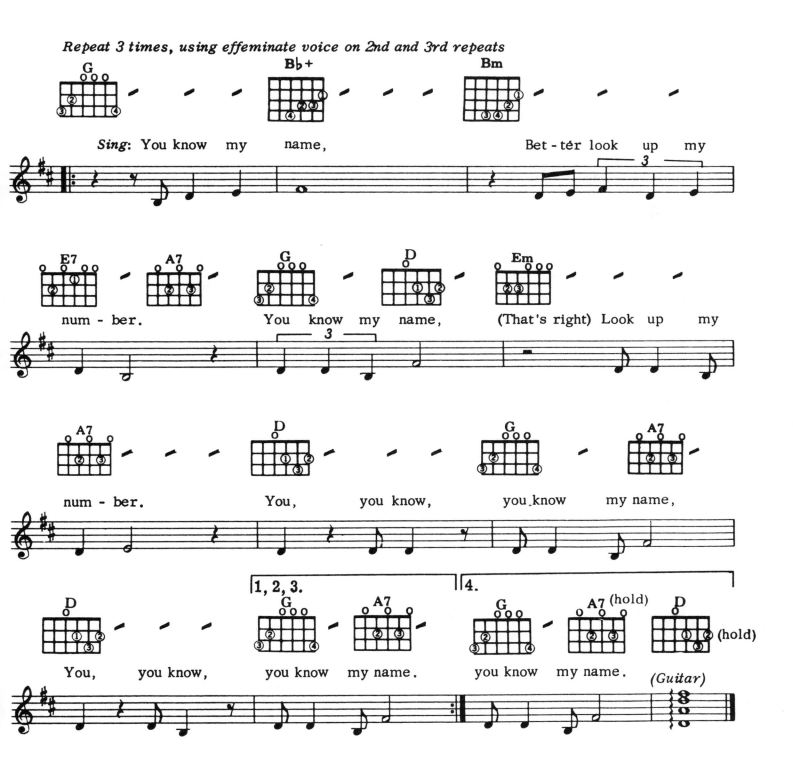

YOU LIKE ME TOO MUCH

By GEORGE HARRISON

Starting note for singing:

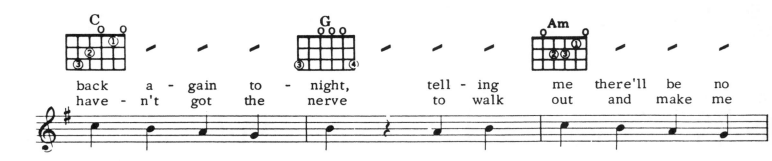

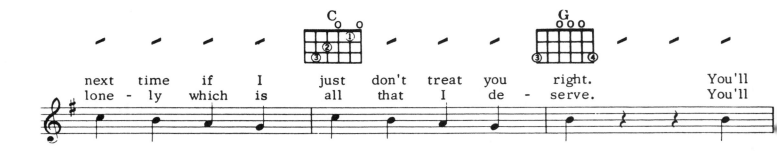

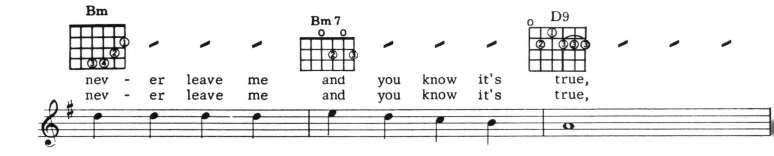

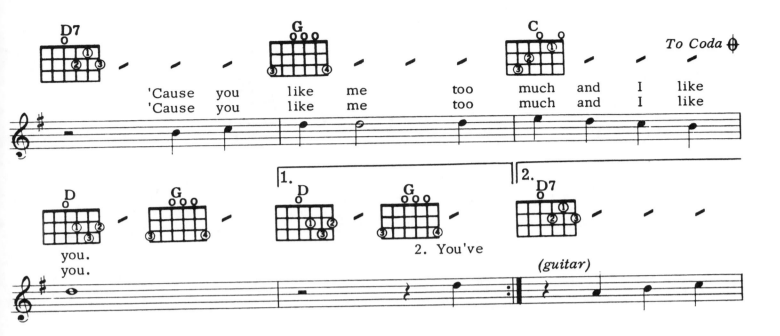

D7   **G**   **C**   *To Coda*

'Cause you like me too much and I like
'Cause you like me too much and I like

D   **G**   **1.** **D**   **G**   **2.** **D7**

you.
you.   2. You've   *(guitar)*

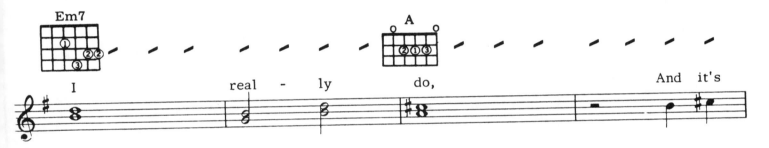

Em7   **A**

I real - ly do, And it's

Bm   **A7**   **Em7**   **A7**

nice when you be - lieve me. If you

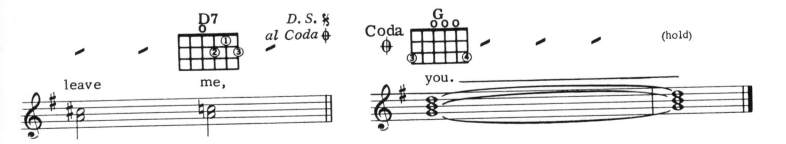

D7   *D. S.*   **Coda**   **G**   *(hold)*
      al Coda

leave me,   you.

3. I will follow you and bring you back where you belong
   'Cause I couldn't really stand it, I admit that I was wrong,
   I wouldn't let you leave me 'cause it's true,
   'Cause you like me too much and I like you.

You Never Give Me Your Money

By JOHN LENNON and PAUL McCARTNEY

YOU WON'T SEE ME

By JOHN LENNON and PAUL McCARTNEY

Starting note
for singing:

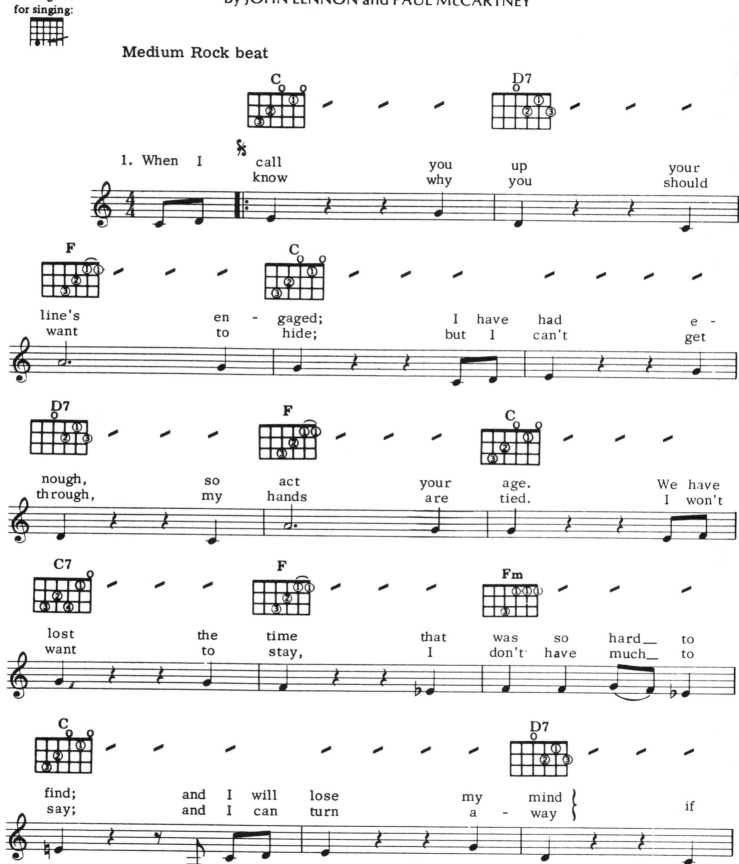

Medium Rock beat

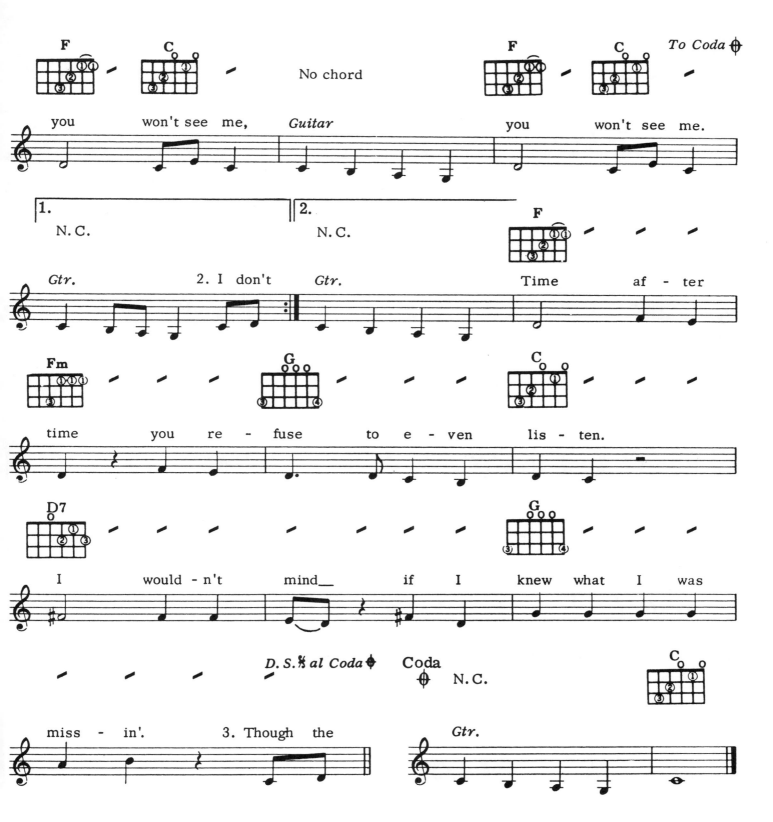

3. Though the days are few, they're filled with tears;
   And since I lost you, it feels like years.
   Yes, it seems so long since you've been gone;
   And I just can't go on
   If you won't see me, you won't see me.

YOUR MOTHER SHOULD KNOW

By JOHN LENNON and PAUL McCARTNEY

Starting note for singing:

Moderately

Am Let's all get up and dance to a song that was a hit be-fore your
Lift up your hearts and sing me a song that was a hit be-fore your

Dm moth-er was born.
moth-er was born.

G7 C Though she was born a long, long time a-

A7 D7 G7 C go, your moth-er should know, your moth-er should know.

1. **E7** Sing it a-gain.

2. **A7 D7** Your moth-er should know,

G7 C E7 Your moth-er should know. *(guitar)*

Am F Dm7 G9 C *(hold)*

You've Got To Hide Your Love Away

By JOHN LENNON and PAUL McCARTNEY

Starting note for singing:

Fast, in 6 (each ♪ = 1 beat)

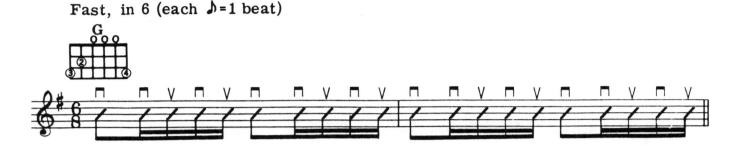

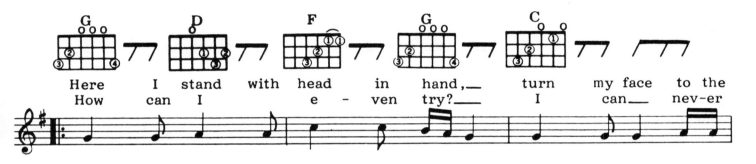

Here I stand with head in hand,___ turn my face to the
How can I e-ven try?___ I can___ nev-er

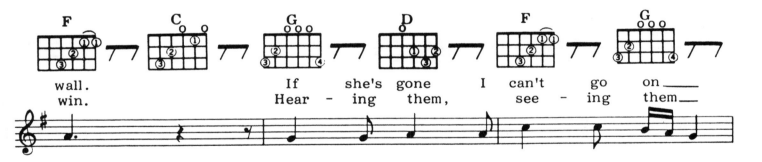

wall. If she's gone I can't go on___
win. Hear-ing them, see-ing them___

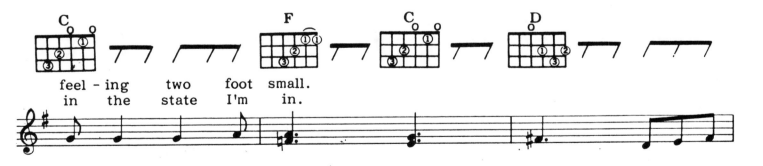

feel-ing two foot small.
in the state I'm in.

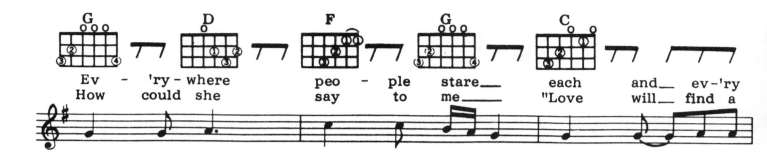

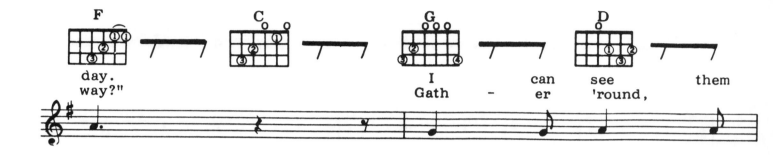

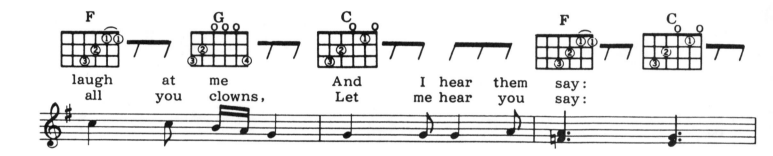

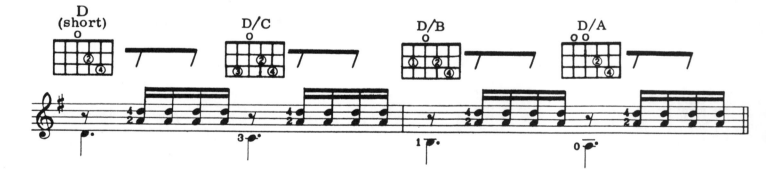

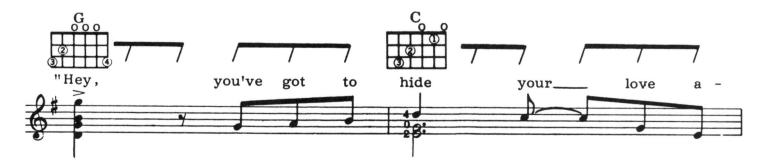

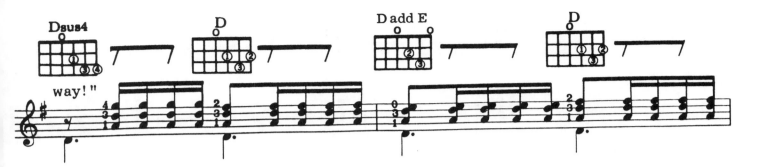

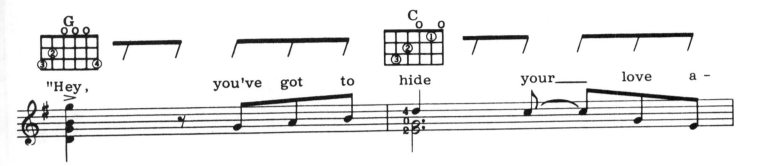

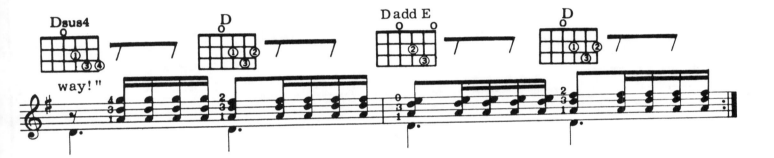

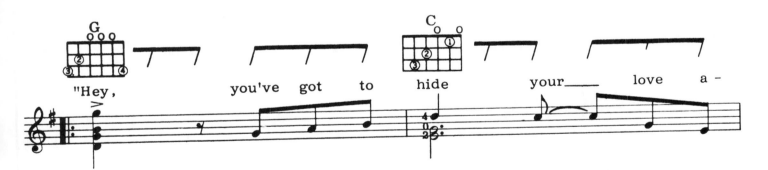

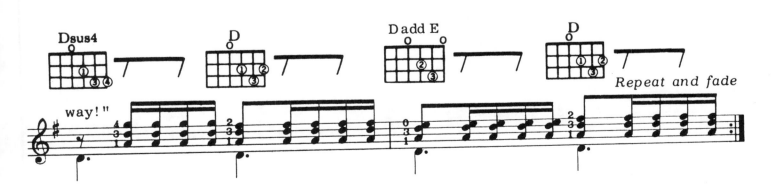

YOU'RE GOING TO LOSE THAT GIRL

By JOHN LENNON and PAUL McCARTNEY

Starting note for singing:

Moderately

You're going to lose that girl, You're going to lose that girl.

If you don't take her out to-night she's going to change her mind,

And I will take her out to-night and I will treat her kind.

You're going to lose that girl, you're going to lose that girl.___

If you don't treat her right, my friend, you're going to find her gone,